READING NABOKOV

READING
NABOKOV

Douglas Fowler

*Cornell
University
Press* | ITHACA
AND
LONDON

First published 1974 by Cornell University Press.
Published in the United Kingdom by Cornell University Press Ltd.,
2–4 Brook Street, London W1Y 1AA.

International Standard Book Number 0–8014–0828–8
Library of Congress Catalog Card Number 73–20798

Printed in the United States of America by York Composition Co., Inc.

For Baxter Hathaway

**MY TEACHER,
FRIEND, AND
CONSCIENCE**

Acknowledgments

I wish to thank Vladimir Nabokov and his publishers for permission to quote from the following works:

Ada, copyright © 1969 by McGraw-Hill International Inc.; *Bend Sinister,* copyright © 1947 by Vladimir Nabokov; "The Room" and "The Ballad of Longwood Glen," from *Poems and Problems,* copyright © 1970 by McGraw-Hill International, Inc. Quotations by permission of McGraw-Hill International, Inc.

Pnin, copyright © 1953, 1955, 1957 by Vladimir Nabokov; quotations by permission of Vladimir Nabokov and Doubleday & Co., Inc. Material from chapter 3 of *Pnin,* copyright © 1954, 1955, 1957 by Vladimir Nabokov, was originally published in *The New Yorker* and is reprinted by permission of Doubleday & Co., Inc. Quotations from "Spring in Fialta" by Vladimir Nabokov, copyright © 1947 by the Hearst Corporation, from the book *Nabokov's Dozen;* by permission of Doubleday & Co., Inc.

Lolita, copyright © 1955 by Vladimir Nabokov; *Pale Fire,* copyright © 1962, and *The Gift,* copyright © 1963, by G. P. Putnam's Sons; quotations by permission of G. P. Putnam's Sons. "Triangle within Circle," reprinted in *The Gift,* was originally published in *The New Yorker,* March 23, 1963.

Lines from T. S. Eliot's "Marina" are reprinted from *Collected*

Poems, 1909–1962 by T. S. Eliot, by permission of Harcourt Brace Jovanovich, Inc., and Faber and Faber, Ltd.

Lines from John Crowe Ransom's "Bells for John Whiteside's Daughter" are reprinted from *Selected Poems* by John Crowe Ransom, third edition, revised and enlarged, copyright © 1962, 1963, 1969 by Alfred A. Knopf, Inc., by permission of Alfred A. Knopf, Inc.

DOUGLAS FOWLER

Tallahassee, Florida

Contents

READING NABOKOV

Introduction:
Nabokov's Constants

This book offers a reading of five of Vladimir Nabokov's novels and three of his short stories, and it refers to a good deal more of his fiction, to his criticism, and to his autobiography. I hope to demonstrate that the fiction is organized about a set of thematic, moral, and narrative constants, and that if we read it with these constants in mind, we will understand it better and enjoy it more.

I begin by taking a close look at *Bend Sinister,* which I believe can serve as a paradigm of Nabokov's methods and intentions. Then, applying the paradigm to each story, I interpret some of the short fiction, hoping to enlarge and refine our reading in a cumulative manner. I follow with a chapter each on *Pale Fire, Pnin, Lolita, Ada,* and, finally, Nabokov's Poem "The Ballad of Longwood Glen."

Although this method should give us Nabokov's fiction in stereoscopic depth and show us those constants at work in each piece, it is dangerous insofar as it tends to produce what might be called "district attorney" criticism: evidence is put forth solely to prove a point, and anything that cannot be used to advance that point is obscured or ignored. A statement from Nabokov's novel *The Gift* is apropos. Speaking of poetry that convinces with its precision and thus earns the reader's trust, Nabokov says that this conviction is generated "not because everything is delineated with an excessively selective touch, but because the presence of the smallest features is involuntarily conveyed to the reader by the integrity and reliability of a talent that assures the author's observance of all the articles of the artistic covenant."[1] If we replace "artistic" with "critical," then I think we must agree that the most important tenet of that reader-critic covenant is honesty. Ignoring or altering the evidence will forfeit the reader's trust and render the evidence useless.

Perhaps the most important constant within Nabokov's longer fiction is the "equivalent"—a character who is a male genius, usually of European birth, and whose capabilities, humor, and taste are such that, as A. C. Bradley pointed out of Prince Hamlet, he could have conceived and written not only the work in which he appears but the rest of the canon as well. In other words, Nabokov creates in his fiction a character who could have created Nabokov's fiction. Nabokov's use of a favorite would not be exceptionally important in itself except for a corollary aspect: unlike Hamlet's evident failures of sexuality, sensibility, and moral obligation, the Nabokovian equivalent is not allowed any failings at all, or only highly specialized ones, like nympholepsy. Nabokov's insistence on the integrity, prejudices, success, brilliance, and moral superiority of the authorial favorite at the expense of all other novelistic considerations creates a radical displacement in the narrative structure that surrounds the favorite, and severely limits the possibilities of narrative development. As I will try to show, Nabokov never sacrifices the perfection of his equivalent to the demands of his story, nor is his favorite allowed any interest in the middling terms of life: money, career, marriage, ambition, institutions, moral choices, failures. None of these are permitted to touch the equivalent. Narrative interest is sometimes supplied by a highly charged melodrama in which the authorial equivalent is only a passive agent, as in *Bend Sinister* or *Invitation to a Beheading;* or the author may invent a pair of monster-clowns who can act in lieu of the equivalent (as Kinbote and Gradus do in *Pale Fire*); or he may create the kind of fiction in which the narrative is atrophied and the reader's interest in it is replaced by an interest in watching the equivalent-as-artist, an engagement in watching the equivalent create art. This sort of engagement we find in most concentrated form in *The Gift* or in the presentation of poet John Shade in *Pale Fire*. Action, then, is in Nabokov an ancillary of character, not its expression. We should look at his narrative construction from this vantage.

Another constant in Nabokov's work is obsessive concern with the prison of human mortality. "Looking at it objectively," Nabokov told an interviewer, "I have never seen a more lucid, more lonely, better balanced mad mind than mine."[2] Perhaps what he describes as "mad" is his refusal to accept the brutal and banal facts of time and death. In his autobiography *Speak, Memory*, Nabokov calls our mortality "the utter degradation, ridicule and horror of having . . . an infinity of sensation and thought within a finite existence,"[3] and this is also the most urgent concern of his fictional favorites: Adam Krug tells us that his "intelligence . . . [cannot] accept the inanity of accumulating incalculable treasures of thought and sensation, and thought-behind-thought and sensation-behind-sensation, to lose them all at once and forever in a fit of black nausea followed by infinite nothingness."[4]

This "mad" concern with the preposterous, "inane" facts of time and death is perhaps the central impulse behind Nabokov's habitual creation of the second world we find in his fiction, of the habitual concern in it with a mode of consciousness or being behind the commonsensical, finite, time-bound one we call real. For example, Krug in *Bend Sinister* seems to be created in the

mode of the usual fictional character. We watch his story proceed
across the verisimilar world of fictional narrative for most of the
novel, only to discover, as Krug himself discovers, that this seemingly commonplace narrative has delivered a set of images and
messages indicating the presence and participation of a transcendent deity in his fate—"a kind of stealthy, abstractly vindictive,
groping, tampering movement that had been going on in a
dream, or behind a dream, in a tangle of immemorial . . . machinations."[5] This mysterious presence is revealed to be Nabokov
himself, the creator of the fiction, Krug's tormentor, and finally
his savior. Nabokov superimposes world on world, for the world
before us is never enough for his equivalents. The refusal to take
this world and its time and death as fatal givens is one of the
sources of Nabokov's most important tension. Van Veen in *Ada*
arrives at the mutant Cartesian formulation, "the final tragic
triumph of human cogitation: I am because I die," and his reaction on being invited to visit the gravesite of Ada's tutor draws
from him the hysteria that we can feel as an undercurrent in
every one of Nabokov's favorites: "You know I abhor church-
yards, I despise, I denounce death, dead bodies are burlesque, I
refuse to stare at a stone under which a roly-poly old Pole is rot-
ting, let him feed his maggots in peace, the entomologies of death
leave me cold, I detest, I despise—" (297).

The brute fact that, yes, we will die is the absurdity from which
Nabokov's art is in part generated—for it is only in art, he believes, that transcendence can be achieved. And even that escape
is only a false solution: Kinbote's madness and the "durable pigments" of art which Humbert creates as a tribute to Lolita and
which is her "only immortality" are neither of them solutions to
time and death, but only temporary escapes, "local palliatives."
Nabokov's characters, like their creator, realize that "the prison
of time is spherical and without exits."[6] But they cannot stop try-

ing to find a means out of time—madness, suicide, nympholepsy, art are the expression of that overmastering impulse to escape. The Nabokovian protagonist is a man in flight, and we must remember this fact when we read.

The reader should qualify Nabokov's claim that in all good fiction, just as in all good chess problems, "the real clash is not between the characters," but between the writer and "the world."[7] This "clash" is part of what Nabokov feels to be the satisfactions a narrative artist can provide us, and the game should never be ignored. There seems to be persuasive evidence, however, that the word-play and the private systems of correspondence and self-reference, the "wayside murmur of this or that hidden theme,"[8] the allusions, recurrent details, anagrams, and triple-tongued puns are annotated red herrings. These curiosities are not in themselves difficult to construct, nor does their solution provide anything much deeper than the solver's thrill, that quite minor delight the crossword-puzzler or Scrabblist derives from his addiction. What is important about them is the *pattern* of "intricate enchantment and deception" they form, which is the signature of the deity who is creating the work. From out of that pattern a coherence does indeed emerge: Nabokov loves an art that mimes as nature does, and he insists on a nature not just brutishly Darwinian but a nature for art's sake, a nature that loves mimicry and disguise. But we should be careful about assigning intrinsic merit to the by-play, as I hope to make clear in my discussions of the recurrent patterns of detail, or "micro-motifs."

The most interesting qualities in Nabokov's novels and stories are the compassion he makes us feel so frequently for his characters; the brilliant use of language (perhaps the most dazzling prose ever written in English); the genius for mimicry and sharp observation; the laughter that isn't forgetful of pain; the tart,

funny, exhilarating combination of elegance and venom; the slap-
stick hilarity. But for those concerns there would be no point in
reading Nabokov at all—a claim that, if true, is largely ignored.

A fourth constant examined here is Nabokov's moral scheme.
He habitually presents himself as a kind of icy-hearted puppeteer
—the "great and inhuman artist," he calls himself repeatedly in
Ada. He keeps insisting that his narrative art has no humanistic
or satirical, and hence corrective or world-mending, interest or
intentions. Indeed, it doesn't. We can agree with Nabokov that
art should always be about the business of expressing its own impulses and arriving at its own truths—and supremely important
ends of art which can only be falsified by didacticism. Nabokov is
so concerned about this falsification that he is even wary of the
term "art for art's sake," since he feels that "such promoters of
it as, for instance, Oscar Wilde and various dainty poets, were in
reality rank moralists and didacticists."[9] But of course, in a puri-
fied state, those words express the notion that the magic of art
lies only in its own inutile firefly impulse, nothing more.

Nabokov's worlds are distinguished from those of most
modern writers by their clear-out moral organization: Good and
the good, and Evil and the evil are absolutely differentiated in his
worlds. Within their own limits, his novels are extraordinarily
pure moral constructions. They are, in fact, fairytales. Even in
Nabokov's greatest and most famous fairytale, the evil is carefully
circumscribed by Humbert's refusal to murder Charlotte, although the motive is enormous and the opportunity purposely
provided. Further, Nabokov ensures that even the lesser evil is
carefully expiated by the novel's structure. The illustration of this
expiation is, I think, important.

There is an extraordinary moral significance in the scene in
which Humbert Humbert confronts the remains of his nymphet,
now hugely pregnant, unkempt, shortly to die in childbirth, a

Mrs. Richard Schiller in an obsure Coalmont somewhere in Universal Appalachia, with her "ruined looks and her adult rope-veined hands." Mrs. Schiller is not his Dolly Haze. She is "pale and polluted and big with another's child," but Humbert can suddenly declare that he "loved her more than anything I had ever seen or imagined on earth, or hoped for anywhere else." Discovering himself in love with a human being rather than simply a nymphet, and declaring his love (it is futile, but no matter), Humbert has not partially discharged for himself (and for the reader) the moral and ethical obligations Nabokov persuaded us to incur when we tacitly approved Humbert's quasi-abduction of a pubescent orphan and of the heartbreaking and hilarious motel-hop they make merely to gratify his perversion. Now, after all that, what he feels is love—and love redeems him. Now Humbert's killing of Quilty can be hilarious and exhilarating because the reader's moral feelings, to say nothing of Humbert's, have been carefully legitimized; Quilty can now be viewed as Humbert's perverted and vicious *Doppelgänger,* whose destruction is desirable. This effect is a result of a careful attention to moral structure characteristic of Nabokov.

When we add in anticipation that Nabokov loathes a number of things—general ideas; any sort of group; abridged dictionaries; symbols of a religious, anthropological, or Freudian sort ("Let the credulous and the vulgar continue to believe that all mental woes can be cured by a daily application of old Greek myths to their private parts. I really do not care");[10] the contributions of Marx, Lenin, and Stalin to the Soviet Union; and the destruction of human freedom and human life—we are ready to begin with *Bend Sinister.* Nabokov's political outlook is summarized by his outburst against the Soviets in the Introduction to *The Waltz Invention:* "It is hard, I submit, to loathe bloodshed, including war, more than I do, but it is still harder to exceed my loathing of the very nature of totalitarian states in which massacre is only an administrative detail."[11] *Bend Sinister* leads us into the totalitarian nightmare, and there we shall set about refining and enlarging our reading of Nabokov.

1

The Nabokov Paradigm:
Bend Sinister

Krug and the Common Man

The novel *Bend Sinister* deals with the rise of a dictator named Paduk in a nameless Central European country whose most famous citizen is the novel's protagonist, the philosopher Adam Krug, a former classmate of Paduk's. Paduk, consolidating and legitimizing his new regime, a regime complete with the new social philosophy "Ekwilism," wants Krug to endorse the government. Krug refuses bribes and resists the adumbration of his own fate as his friends are arrested one by one, but he is finally "convinced" when his son David is taken from him and he himself is arrested. Although Krug has capitulated in order to save his son, some offstage bungling on the part of David's guards results in the little boy's being taken to a hospital for the criminally insane, where he is used as a "hostility-conductor" and killed in the process. Krug's wife Olga is dying of complications from an automobile accident when the novel opens, and Adam himself soon joins the rest of his family in death when, transported by insanity past all recognition of time past and time present and believing himself back in his school days, he tries to bully Puduk as he did then and is killed by the dictator's bodyguards. This is a summary of the novel's action as that term applies to the fictional characters operating on a consistent fictional plane. The novel's complexities, unlike those of *Lolita* or *Ada,* have little to do with the narrative action.

Nabokov always contrasts isolated genius with collective imbecility, and his heroes are always threatened by a group. The reader should never forget to oversimplify along with Nabokov in order to read him accurately: the solitary genius is absolutely good, the group absolutely evil. But if the equivalent character is superior to the group which threatens him, he is also vulnerable in a way that the members of the group are not. The opening incidents of *Bend Sinister* present this contrast vividly and characteristically. Krug is trying to return home to his son, for his wife has just died in Prinzin Hospital and he is stopped by Paduk's soldiers after crossing a bridge.

"Aren't you lowering to a considerable extent the standards by which the function, if any, of the human brain is judged?" (13) Krug asks the guards who would have him return to the other side of the bridge for a "necessary" signature, necessary because that is the rule. The answer is a hymn to the instinct of the bureau: "When you come back again with your pass signed and everything in order—think of the inner satisfaction you will feel when we countersign it . . . and anyway, we should not shirk a certain amount of physical exertion if we want to be worthy of our Ruler," (13) he is told. So there is nothing for it— Krug obeys the instructions and a good-burgher philistine of the sort who create the milieu in which fascism thrives accompanies him back across the bridge. Krug's "delightful companion" delivers to us a précis of everything Nabokov abominates about the values of the universal middle class and everything that he feels makes movements like Hitler's successful. The Nazi crimes, Nabokov reminds us, cannot be dismissed as crimes that occured only in the past in "remote khanates and mandarinates";[1] they are committed in the present, in front of us, with the consent of the

average man. Krug's "delightful companion" is that average
man: " 'Less books and more commonsense—that's my motto.
People are made to live together . . . and not sit alone, thinking dangerous thoughts. . . . Teach young people to count, to
spell, to tie a parcel, to be tidy and polite, to take a bath every
Saturday, to speak to prospective buyers' " (18). The special
appeal of Ekwilism lies not in any practical effect it may have
upon the social organism or the economy but in its enforcement
of the idea of equality, an equality so absolute that it requires the
extinction of all human differences.

Although Krug's companion is obviously used to furnish ludicrous testimony against himself, what is less obvious is Nabokov's
almost masochistic insistence on having the man judge everything
in terms of its utility: " ' I have been told by a reliable person
that in one bookshop there actually is a book of at least a hundred
pages which is wholly devoted to the anatomy of bedbugs' " (18),
he says to Krug, just to share the horror. Contrast this with what
Nabokov himself proudly relates in an interview: "My names
for the microscopic organs [of butterflies] that I have been the
first to see and portray have safely found their way into the
biological dictionaries."[2] Krug, a Nabokov equivalent, esteems
his colleagues " 'because they are able to find perfect felicity in
specialized knowledge and because they are not apt to commit
physical murder' " (52). A sometimes xenophobic strain of individuality differentiates first-rate characters from inferior ones in
all Nabokov's work, and none of his heros is a joiner or a good
companion in even a minimal sense, or one of "all those who *are*
because they do *not* think, thus refuting Cartesianism" (10).

Krug, imprisoned in a segment of time and fast moving further
and further beyond the moment of Olga's death, wishes he had
had the opportunity "of stopping this or that bit of our common
life, prophylactically, prophetically, letting this or that moment

rest in peace. Taming time . . . pampering life—our patient
. . . [immobilizing] by this . . . method millions of moments;
paying perhaps terrific fines, but stopping the train" (11). By
esthetic if not by rational law, shouldn't this be possible?

Nabokov's sense of the miraculousness and fragility of human
life is explicit in *Speak, Memory:* "Nature expects a full-grown
man to accept the two black voids, fore and aft, as stolidly as he
accepts the extraordinary visions in between. . . . I feel the urge
to take my rebellion outside and picket nature."³ Nabokov calls
himself a "chronophobiac." "Over and over again, my mind has
made colossal efforts to distinguish the faintest of personal glim-
mers in the impersonal darkness on both sides of my life," he confesses. "That this darkness is caused merely by the walls of time
separating me and my bruised fists from the free world of timelessness is a belief I gladly share with the most gaudily painted
savage."⁴ The "merely" in this sentence expresses the outrage
that is Nabokov's own characteristic reaction to the vulnerability
of human consciousness.

It is not much of a surprise that the suffering Krug and his
babbling companion arrive finally at the end of the rebridged
bridge and find no one there to stop them or even to check their
passes; the pointlessness is the point. The game's rules are wholly
arbitrary. Krug's tragedy is to ignore the fact that, although the
rules are wholly arbitrary and almost entirely nonsense, they are
relentlessly enforced.

Quality and Quantity

T. S. Eliot once called fascism "only the extreme degradation
of democracy," a phrase that describes the philosophy of Ekwilism
even more perfectly. Nearly every tenet of Ekwilism is an anath-
ema to a mind and personality like Nabokov's—and, of course,
to Krug's.

The last semester of Krug's high-school days had been marked by the sudden rise of Paduk, called by his school fellows "the Toad," battered but persistent object of relentless bullying, which included the daily ordeal of having Krug sit on his face. During the semester Paduk founds the first Party of the Average Man and surrounds himself with a retinue: "Every one of his followers had some little defect or 'background of security' as an educationist after a fruit cocktail might put it: one boy suffered from permanent boils, another was morbidly shy, a third had by accident beheaded his baby sister, a fourth stuttered so badly that you could go out and buy yourself a chocolate bar while he was wrestling with an initial *p* or *b*" (65).

Paduk's father, an eccentric inventor and printer of social tracts, had become acquainted with the philosophical fountainhead of Ekwilism, Fradrik Skotoma. "[Skotoma] introduced the idea of balance as a basis for universal bliss . . . [but] prudently omitted to define both the practical method to be pursued and the kind of person or persons responsibile for planning and directing the process" (67). Paduk and his schoolboy cronies take up a garbled form the Skotoma's thought and garble it further, then join Skotoma's philosophy of "balance"—equalization of the "spiritual liquid" of human consciousness—with a newspaper cartoon character, Mr. Etermon (Everyman), and evolve their version of the ideal citizen. It is toward Mr. Etermon that Ekwilism will conduct us: "Mr. Etermon taking a z-nap on the divan or stealing into the kitchen to sniff with erotic avidity the sizzling stew, represented quite unconsciously a living refutation of individual immortality, since his whole habitus was a dead-end with nothing in it capable or worthy of transcending the mortal condition" (68).

Nabokov and Krug realize how infinite human consciousness is, Paduk and the citizen on the bridge suppress that realization in the interests of conformity to the tenets of a social philosophy.

The label "Ekwilism" is of course only the sketchiest equivalent of the metaphysics of Hitler's national socialism or Lenin's communism. In fact, Nabokov acknowledges his debt in the introduction with his characteristic graciousness toward those orthodoxies: "Idiotic and despicable regimes . . . worlds of tyranny and torture, of Fascist and Bolshevists, of philistine thinkers and jackbooted baboons . . . without those infamous models before me I could not have interlarded this fantasy with bits of Lenin's speeches, and a chunk of the Soviet constitution, and gobs of Nazist pseudoefficiency" (xiii). Paduk, ridding himself of the possibilities and conflicts of the human personality, reducing himself into an outline, copies the Etermon cartoon even down to aspects of grooming and clothing. Paduk's self-reduction draws Nabokov's satirical savagery and represents his hositility to social philosophy, simplistic ideas, and the communal instinct. Nabokov's disgust with the self-imposed limitations necessary to most social philosophies sets him apart with the characters who closely resemble himself.

Nabokov's Favoritism

One of the remarkable aspects of Nabokov's fiction is the degree to which he indulges in shameless favoritism for his author-equivalent characters, especially in matters of intelligence, taste, and what might euphemistically be termed "genetic possibility." Krug's father was "a biologist of considerable repute"—pure rather than applied science is a favored positive value everywhere in Nabokov—whereas Paduk's father is a wholly marginal creature, "a minor inventor, a vegetarian, a theosophist, a great expert in cheap Hindu lore; at one time . . . in the printing business —printing mainly the works of cranks and frustrated politicians" (59). And he represents the healthier side of Paduk's family. His mother is described as "a flaccid lymphatic [who] died in child-birth." Paduk's father, however, marries again, this time "a young cripple for whom he had been devising a new type of braces (she survived him, braces and all, and is still limping about somewhere)" (59).

Nabokov is never "fair" in his fiction, and the distortions created by his author-equivalents generate problems for the "over-voice"—the voice in which the story is told—as well as for the characterizations and the plot. One example of this favoritism in *Bend Sinister* occurs when Krug is taken by chauffeured limou-sine to a conference of frightened university professors, who are all to sign loyalty oaths to the "bloated and dangerously divine State" under the eyes of Dr. Azureus, president of the university, and a certain "Dr. Alexander," described as "one of those people who in times of disaster emerge from dull obscurity to blossom forth suddenly with permits, passes, coupons, cars, connections, lists of addresses" (31), and who proves of course to be Paduk's spy.

Krug is alone with his "dead wife and sleeping child" in the midst of these third-raters, but Nabokov, finding in the necessity of creating a few scraps of plausible academic conversation an op-portunity to demonstrate to us the quality of Krug's thinking, seizes on three bystanding nonentities: a professor of modern history states, apropos of nothing, that the "recurrent combina-tions" of history are "perceptible as such only . . . when they are imprisoned so to speak in the past. . . . To try to map our tomorrows with the help of data supplied by our yesterdays means ignoring the basic element of the future which is its complete non-existence" (39). Since this aperçu is evidently a profundity of which Nabokov approves (it is also dressed in the telltale metaphoric elegance he reserves for his overvoice and author-equivalents: History is "Clio" and "my client," and she "cannot

repeat herself" because her "memory is too short," and so on)`,
it cannot simply be given away indiscriminately to a "Professor
of History" who is not named, described, or seen again, so Nabokov has an even more transparent "Professor of Economics"
murmur the phrase "pure Krugism" in a voice audible only to
the reader.

A casual authorial interruption turns our attention away from
the summary dismissal of these characters, but the point should
not be missed that Nabokov ignores the sorrowing of his "favorite
character" (as he nakedly announces of his feelings toward
Krug) in order to bring on stage more evidence of that character's extraordinary superiority to the rest of the cast.

The reader of Nabokov must identify the field of force between author and favorite character before the rest of the fiction
can be clearly experienced. To further complicate matters, Nabokov does not always use the author–favorite character relationship
to supply the energy from which the foreground activity is generated; for example, in *Pnin* the title role is not taken by the
author, for he contents himself with the briefer role of Victor
Wind, and although the Nabokov-Victor relationship is powerful, it is secondary and subtle, and allows Pnin himself to be the
delightful victim-buffoon that he is; and John Shade in *Pale Fire*
occupies a role secondary to that of the monstrous pedant-pervert
Kinbote, limited as the great old poet is to creation—not at all
the same thing as action.

Ignoring the Middle Ground

If a writer creates for the protagonist of his fiction a character
who resembles Vladimir Nabokov, he severely limits for himself
the kind of story that he can tell. Nabokov is a good example of
a writer who chose that subject and those limitations, and his
fiction shows the narrative possibilities into which he has con-
strained himself as a result.

One working rule for looking at fiction might postulate that the "middle ground" of the novelist's narrative possibilities— money, marriages, social distinction, minor epiphany, lessons learned about the implications inherent in the possibilites of civilized choice or institutions—this commonsensical and "realistic" plane, the plane of Dickens or of James or Cozzens or Anthony Powell and even Fitzgerald, demands a protagonist interested in and affected by those terms. For example, the possibilities of society are very real to a Dick Diver, and even if he eventually wears through them into a nihilism that exhausts and destroys those possibilities, this nihilism does not trivialize them. In Fitzgerald, the green dock lights go off one by one, the count of enchanted objects can diminish and never increase, but the game is the game, and Fitzgerald is very tough with his characters on that score. But the Nabokovian protagonist is never involved in a game in which the values of society play any positive part, and the similarities of two books as objectively dissimilar as *The Gift* and *Bend Sinister* are partially a result of the impasse Nabokov creates for himself with his astonishingly brilliant, erudite, sophisticated, self-determining protagonists.

Donald Malcolm noted that the émigré protagonist of *The Gift,* an obvious Nabokov-equivalent character called Fyodor Godunov-Cherdyntsev, limits and displaces all the usual concerns of novelistic narrative. "[Fyodor's] insatiable eye devours whole landscapes of asphalt and wallpaper"[5] Malcolm says, and praises the novel's extraordinary sensuous brilliance. But Malcolm also notes the "boredom of surfeit" in the enormous mass of motiveless yet detailed description and in the inclusion, by Nabokov, of a very real biography of the Russian liberal writer Chernyshevski "written" by Fyodor—a biography thorough and uncompromising and realistic enough to have been deleted from the novel when it was serialized in the émigré Russian paper *Sovremennye Zapiski* in Berlin in the thirties. Malcolm points out that Nabokov

"imperturbably maintains a constant tenuity of connection between impulse and action, circumstance and consequence, that
is more common to the diffusions of actuality than to the rigors of
art," and he compares its diffusions unfavorably to *Lolita*, which
he calls "a triumph of coherent art" largely because of "the singular power of this novel's crucial relationship . . . which impels
every fragment into alignment."

Bend Sinister, like *Lolita*, depends for its dynamic on a "crucial
relationship," this one not of love but of terror: Paduk must be
Paduk, not only as an expression of Nabokov's conceptual bias
but also as a matter of narrative necessity. If Nabokov and those
creations of his nearest to him cannot interest themselves in the
commonsensical middle ground, then they must be delivered to
the extremes of motionless sensibility or to melodrama, and these
alternatives, because they ignore the usual concerns of narrative,
resemble each other more than they resemble that commonsensical middle ground. The extraordinary quantity and quality of
violence in Nabokov's work doubtless derives from the deepest
springs of his experience; but, in another sense, that violence is the
inevitable outcome of the unreconcilable disparity between the
camp of the protagonist and the camp of the others, where it is
much darker and all the sounds and smells and sights are tinged
with horror and disgust. Nabokov's fiction is frequently almost at
the mercy of the crisis it creates for itself by ranging the marvelous against the monstrous again and again. The relationship between them can only be that of predator and victim.

Paduk, Krug, and Nabokov

Paduk is not clearly realized as a character, and this faulty
characterization is neither a matter of Nabokov's inability to
render viciousness convincing—he in fact does so with several of
Paduk's henchmen—nor is it a matter of his not finding Paduk

as monster interesting. The blurriness seems to proceed from an authorial insistence that Paduk be misshapen in ways that include too many of Nabokov's own anathemas, and from a failure to fuse the disparate elements in Paduk's character—his sexual inversion, obsessive fixation, and intellectual mediocrity.

We would expect to find in the schoolboy an embryo of the later monstrosity, but Nabokov's presentation of the young Paduk is not adequate to the reptilian tyrant he later becomes. "[He] had an irritating trick of calling his classmates by anagrams of their names . . . this he did not from any sense of humor, which he totally lacked, but because, as he carefully explained . . . all men consist of the same twenty-five letters variously mixed" (60). Doubtless Nabokov omits "I" from Paduk's alphabetical count, but the real point of this habit of Paduk's is to demonstrate his commitment to total equalization by the breaking down of all individuality into its common components. And as a thumbnail metaphor for Paduk's dogma of self-annihilation, Nabokov gives us the "padograph."

The padograph is a typewriter-like invention of Paduk's father and reproduces "with repellent perfection the hand of its owner" (60). It brings some commercial success to Paduk père, but its function for Nabokov and the reader is metaphoric: "Philosophically speaking, the padograph subsisted as an Ekwilist symbol, as a proof of the fact that a mechanical device can reproduce personality, and the Quality is merely the distribution aspect of Quantity" (61). The last phrase is, of course, the item nearest Paduk's heart and hence furthest from Nabokov's.

Nabokov is not primarily trying to define either Paduk or a Padukian type but is establishing a connection between Krug and the creator who stands above the fiction, Nabokov himself. The novel must be read simultaneously as linear narrative and stereoscopic artifact. We must read along, and we must read through.

The padograph reminds us of that duality, for the metaphor is not exhausted in merely setting up the essential contrast between the uniqueness of the real human being that Nabokov and Krug believe in and the human-being-as-quantitative-unit postulated by Ekwilism. We learn that Paduk "had never got rid of infantile inkstains, so his father had thrown in additional keys for an hourglass-shaped blot and two round ones. These adornments, however, Paduk ignored, and quite rightly" (61).

The "hourglass-shaped blot," we are informed in the Introduction, appears seven times in the novel and serves as a mediational signal, half comprehended by Krug, which allows Krug's plane and that of the author who has created him a means of interpenetration. "This little puddle vaguely evokes in [Krug] my link with him: a rent in his world leading to another world of tenderness, brightness and beauty" (xv), Nabokov explains, and categorizes his authorial role as that of an "anthropomorphic deity." Naturally then, Paduk cannot concern himself with that inkstain key: Nabokov's esthetic and moral prejudices simply will not make available to the bestial, the mediocre, the unredeemed access to the world one step, one secret above their own. But for those for whom he is like God, the characters he loves, Nabokov provides a spiritual and temporal alternative, a heavenly kingdom or superworld beyond the plane of "reality" in which they, as created characters, exist. Nabokov is in fact more generous than God has been with him and with the rest of us on the plane in which we live. The superworld above the fictional world is the equivalent of the "world of timelessness" that Nabokov himself feels must be right behind the wall of time that surrounds our mortal world, or at least would be behind it if esthetics or ethics could alter the brutal mysteries of life and death. In *Speak, Memory* Nabokov again and again indicates the absurdity of life's wastefulness in creating these marvelous human sensibilities that gather "an infinity of sensation and thought within a finite existence," and the feeling is frequently mystical:

Whenever in my dreams I see the dead, they always appear silent, bothered, strangely depressed, quite unlike their dear, bright selves. I am aware of them, without any astonishment, in surroundings they never visited during their earthly existence. . . . They sit apart, frowning at the floor, as if death were a dark taint, a shameful family secret. It is certainly not them—not in dreams—but when one is wide awake, at moments of robust joy and achievement, on the highest terrace of consciousness, that mortality has a chance to peer beyond its own limits. . . . And although nothing much can be seen through the mist, there is somehow the blissful feeling that one is looking in the right direction.[6]

Despite the artificial tone in which it is sometimes expressed, the feeling is real for Nabokov and forms one of the most powerful subcurrents in *Bend Sinister*. When Krug sleeps, he is possessed and made aware of a deity above him, Nabokov himself: "A nameless, mysterious genius [had taken] advantage of the dream to convey his own peculiar code message . . . which links [Krug] up with an unfathomable mode of being, perhaps terrible, perhaps blissful, perhaps neither, a kind of transcendental madness which lurks behind the corner of consciousness" (56).

Krug and Paduk, now full-grown, now philosopher and dictator, confront each other directly for the first time in chapter 11, but since a clash between Krug and Paduk would be wholly obligatory in the usual screen or novel narrative, Nabokov prefers to explode the device under controlled conditions rather than run the risk of marring the surface of his scene with an irrelevant genre effect going off out of his control. Paduk is physically repulsive, one detail of his repulsiveness being a Nabokovian favorite: "One wondered what tremendous will power a man must possess to refrain from squeezing out the blackheads that clogged the coarse pores on and near the wings of his fattish nose" (127). The description continues in this vein until Nabokov suddenly tries to cancel Paduk. "He was a little too repulsive to be credible, and so let us ring the bell (held by a bronze eagle) and have him beautified by mortician" (128); but even this digression of the author's does not seem to provide either effective beautification for Paduk or, more important, effective escape for Krug from Paduk and his type, or from a hideous fate.

Nabokov tries to convince us that the dictator is morbidly embarrassed to be in the same room with his old classmate Adam Krug, but embarrassment is perhaps the emotion we would be least likely to associate with any of the murderous scramblers who contrive and execute revolutions. Nabokov is evidently more interested in demonstrating Krug's superiority to Paduk than in creating any facsimile of the totalitarian personality, and this preference is quite typical of his fundamental insistence upon an art of elegant esthetics and visible control rather than one of authorial invisibility.

In their short interchange Paduk calls Adam Krug "Mugakrad," "Gumakrad," and "Gumradka"; he also calls him "mad Adam," which reads the same forward and backward. This is an obvious analogue of his penchant for the reorganization of human relationships through reduction and simplification, with the reassembly of those relationships being only a matter of mechanical reorganization of quantitative units. The interview comes to nothing. Any real threat against David would force Krug to capitulate, as he does instantly and without reservation once David is kidnapped, but there is no threat here. The scene, despite its indifference to what we would imagine a "real" confrontation to be, is revealing in regard to the "anthropomorphic deity" Nabokov is impersonating. It is as if the author is especially interested in seeing that Krug does not have to face Paduk alone. This kind of favoritism is central to Nabokov's feelings about his author-equivalent protagonists. We shall see it again during Pnin's worst moment.

The action on the narrative plane is enfeebled by Nabokov's revulsion for what an actual Paduk would look like and sound like, the way he would hate—and this revulsion is in itself an example of the powerful and partisan feelings Nabokov has for the creatures that he makes walk and talk and love and die. But not only does he keep disconnecting the source of fictional verisimilitude by commenting on the credibility of what we are watching, he abruptly changes to an authorial camera angle—that of the "anthropomorphic deity" who is creating the fiction: "Photographed from above, [Krug and Paduk] would have come out in Chinese perspective, doll-like . . . and the secret spectator (some anthropomorphic deity, for example) surely would be amused by the shape of human heads seen from above" (131).

Hints of Paduk's sexual failings flash by: he has a picture postcard of Gainsborough's "Blue Boy" and a "framed reproduction of Aldobrandini's 'Wedding,' of the half-naked wreathed, adorable minion whom the groom is obliged to renounce for the sake of a lumpy, muffled-up bride" (133). Again, this reproduction is far more a signal from Nabokov through his overvoice than a convincing artifact of Paduk's, for not only is a lush Renaissance "decadent" obviously Nabokov's idea of elegant debauchery and perversion rather than a dictator's, but the picture's whole atmosphere of sweet feigning and delicious melancholy is false to what we feel about the fascist-militarist mentality.

Nabokov manifests himself to us and at least obliquely to Krug by signaling through the shape of some spilled milk on Paduk's desk, a "kidney-shaped white puddle," the point of contact between the created world and the world above it. The scene is further reduced by the overvoice which mocks the commonality, grossness, and "simplification" of Ekwilism and once again breaks the narrative verisimilitudes: "Did Krug really glance at the prepared speech? And if he did, was it really as silly as all that? He did; it was" (135). But although the confrontation terminates indecisively on the narrative level, with Krug still convinced that "nothing harmful could happen," the very worst will come to pass. In Nabokov's created worlds, the most sensitive can never escape.

Us and Them

Nabokov's powers of observation and animation in respect to the secondary characters in his fiction are as impressive as he cares to make them. The people, loved or loathed, who occupy positions of emotional or thematic significance but are not in themselves crucial to the central activity in a Nabokov novel, are almost always vivid and convincing. Joan Clements in *Pnin*, Charlotte Haze in *Lolita*, Rodion in *Invitation to a Beheading*, and here in *Bend Sinister*, David, Krug's friend Ember, and Mariette, a police spy who becomes the Krug housekeeper, all share the vitality Nabokov achieves so masterfully when he isn't concerned with creating genius-heroes or monster-clowns.

When at last Paduk sees that the only way of enlisting Krug's public support for his regime is to kidnap David, Krug is separated from the child by Mariette Bachofen, her policewoman sister Linda, and Mac, a super-SS operator whose palm is the size "of a steak for five" and who, in the course of abducting David from Krug, uses "professional precision and *savoir-faire*" to deal the lunging father "a cutting backhand blow with the edge of his pig-iron paw" (179). Nabokov does not merely present this manhandling as a demonstration of fascist physicality; the pig-iron paws and karate serve as backdrop for the more revealing insight into the totalitarian sensibility, the strain of passionless, mildly appreciative, blankly polite indifference to violence exhibited by Mariette and her sister.

"Tell me some more about Hustav," asked Mariette. "How was he strangled?" [Hustav was Linda's fiance, and a few days before he and Linda had arrested Krug's friend Ember in Krug's presence.] "Well, it was like this. They came by the back door while I was making breakfast and said they had instructions to get rid of him. I said aha but I don't want any mess on the floor and I don't want any shooting. . . . I said, I don't want to see you guys doing it and I don't want to spend all day cleaning up. So they took him to the bathroom and started to work on him there. Of course, my morning was ruined. I had to be at my dentist's at ten, and there they were in the bathroom making simply hideous noises—especially Hustav. They must have been at it for at least twenty minutes. He had an Adam's apple as hard as a heel, they said—and of course I was late." [185–186]

When Linda has assisted in Ember's arrest, Krug, furious and disgusted, accuses her of the theft of a little porcelain owl, and his accusation touches a sensitive nerve, peculiar to the law-abiding Nazi: " 'Professor, we are not thieves,' she said very quietly, and he must have had a heart of stone who would not have felt ashamed of his evil thought. . . . The girl came towards him again and opened her white bag to show him she had not purloined anything of real or sentimental value" (113).

Except, of course, David's life, it turns out. But during his separation from his father, Linda ignores the child's helplessness and fright to remind Krug of his impolite error in accusing her of petty theft.

"My dear man," said Linda, "we quite understand that it is your child, or at least your late wife's child, and not a little owl of porcelain or something, but our duty is to take you away and the rest does not concern us." [181]

"Put out the lights, Mariette," said Linda, "or we shall be accused of stealing this man's electricity." [181]

In Nabokov, the excellent are frequently rude and mocking, the evil quite often scrupulously polite and proper. The bureaucrats who support Paduk have substituted propriety for thinking and feeling, and they are acutely conscious of social formulas; these formulas are not masks, but represent a profound and necessary hierarchical system, the violation of which fills them with real pain. During the Krug-Paduk interview, for example, the concern of the electronic eavesdroppers who interrupt Krug's exchange with Paduk is with the strict observance of the proper method of addressing the dictator. This concern is again seen in Linda's indignation at being thought a petty thief. These are essential and relevant insights into the bourgeois-totalitarian mentality in the total State. All the small distinctions are magnified, while all humane feelings—tenderness, curiosity, compassion, empathy—are atrophied. The fascist personality is not cunning or energetic or apocalyptic or even venomous. It is simply incapable of understanding any real system of values, feeling, or esthetics, and it has absolutely no sense of proportion.

This inversion of values reaches its horrifying conclusion as we discover with Krug that David has been mistakenly delivered to the inmates of an "Institute for Abnormal Children"; the error is explained to Krug: "The theory . . . was that if once a week the really difficult patients could enjoy the possibility of venting in full their repressed yearnings . . . upon some little human creature of no value to the community, then, by degrees, the evil in them would be allowed to escape" (195–196).

Once again, Nabokov slightly alters for ironic comment the relatively authentic Nazi "science" to conform with the novel's primary thematic opposition: the individual as opposed to the collective. "After a while the . . . 'inmates' were let into the enclosure. At first they kept at a distance, eyeing the 'little person.' It was interesting to observe how the 'gang' spirit gradually asserted itself. They had been rough lawless unorganized individuals, but now something was binding them, the community spirit (positive) was conquering the individual whims (negative); for the first time in their lives they were *organized*" (196).

Krug, not yet knowing his son is dead, is driven to the Institute by the functionary Crystalsen, whose fear and embarrassment at the bungling fail to mask his pride in the Institute's role in creating a new social order.

Led by a "Dr. Hammecke" (this is, after all, the most Teutonic section of the novel), the tragic farce plays itself out.

A film of "Test 656" is shown; it is silent and subtitled. When the inscription "humorously" requests "No Whistling, Please!" as Frau Doktor von Wytwyl, the third Bachofen sister, appears on the screen, "in spite of the dreadful predicament he was in, even Dr. Hammecke could not restrain an appreciative ha-ha" (200). But when David appears in the film being gently coaxed to his death by a nurse, the reel is stopped and Krug is ushered to a hospital room to see his child. A few pages earlier, Krug has been reunited after his capitulation with what the functionaries had believed to be his real son, but who had turned out to be an "Arvid Krug, son of Professor Martin Krug, former Vice-President of the Academy of Medicine"; the anagrammatic jumble of "David" in the first name is of course another signal of that interchangeability of units that is the first principle of Ekwilism. But here at the Institute there is no mistake. Krug, like all of Nabokov's equivalents, must see the worst.

At the moment when Krug is shown his dead son, the overvoice in which the novel is told becomes unable to decipher the chaotic disintegration of Krug's mind, and square brackets enclose the overvoice's scholarly guesswork amid the agonized babble. "Here the long hand of life becomes extremely illegible" (202), the overvoice carefully notes, and there is another reference to an "inner spy" that Krug had sensed fleetingly before inside his own consciousness while his wife was dying. The overvoice informs us that the sense of this "inner spy" is "not at all clear," but a translation of a fragment of babble identifies Crystalsen (the name suggests the transparency Nabokov despises) as merely one more hallucination "among the subjects of his dreamlike state." These hallucinations prove to be an accurate definition of what all of Krug's tormentors turn out to be, "illusions oppressive to [him] during his brief spell of being, but harmlessly fading away when I dismiss the cast" (xiv). *Bend Sinister* is, after all, only a work of fiction. And there is, after all, a creator one step above Krug who incarnates himself in the novel's last passage while the "cast" is reduced to his "whims and megrims," a cast whose only existence is on the "chaos of written and rewritten pages" (216). But part of Nabokov's meaning is that Krug's fictionality is less a reduction than a salvation, less a diminishment to ink and paper than a flight to a second, and better, world.

At the moment of Krug's terrible discovery of his son's death, the overvoice, the voice of the "anthropomorphic deity," assumes attributes and possibilities quite different from those found elsewhere in the book. It is revealing to look at this metamorphosis more carefully, for this passage is the only one in the novel with which the overvoice confesses having any difficulty in interpretation, or indeed, in penetration. And if the overvoice is the voice of the creator, why then cannot the creator understand his own creation?

The answer perhaps begins with the recognition that Krug's mind and his power to react have been destroyed by the enormous absurdity of bearing infinite pain within a finite consciousness. Nabokov always presents reality as lethal, and all of his favorites are either destroyed by it or in flight from it. Pnin's experience with reality is also represented as unsupportable. During a holiday at a retreat owned by an émigré friend, Pnin experiences once again the death of his beloved Mira Belochkin in a Nazi concentration camp:

What chatty Madam Shpolyanski mentioned had conjured up Mira's image with unusual force. This was disturbing. Only in the detachment of an incurable complaint, in the sanity of near death, could one hope to cope with this for a moment. In order to exist rationally, Pnin had taught himself, during the last ten years, never to remember Mira Belochkin—not because, in itself, the evocation of a youthful love affair, banal and brief, threatened his peace of mind . . . but because, if one were quite sincere with oneself, no conscience, and hence no consciousness, could be expected to subsist in a world where such things as Mira's death were possible. One had to forget—because one could not live with the thought that this graceful, fragile, tender young woman with those eyes, that smile, those gardens and snows in the background, had been brought in a cattle car to an extermination camp and killed by an injection of phenol into the heart, into the gentle heart one had heard beating under one's lips in the dusk of the past. [134–135]

The essential supposition in this passage is that certain kinds of recognition are annihilating. Pnin can, to some extent, shield his consciousness from the recognition that would extinguish it. Krug cannot, and his rational consciousness, which could only be an instrument of unspeakable torture, is at last destroyed by the deity: he is allowed to go mad and escape. "I felt a pang of pity for Adam and slid towards him along an inclined beam of pale light—causing instantaneous madness, but at least saving him from the senseless agony of his logical fate" (210).

In the passage quoted from *Pnin,* the fusion of esthetics and ethics is characteristic, for Nabokov's esthetic is not separable from his moral sense. "Conscience," a moral term, is wholly co-ordinated with the esthetic terms "graceful," "fragile," and with "those eyes" and "that smile." In Nabokov's worlds, the powers of suffering as well as those of love are most prodigious in those with the greatest range of sensibility, with the most powerful sense of the possibilities of consciousness. And in all of Nabokov's fiction, the worst blows fall on those capable of the most suffering. The best fare worst.

Robert M. Adams remarks that "Nabokov's world consists of flats, façades, transparencies; as for the moral and human dimensions—'profundities,' compassions, inner developments—it simply does not have them."[7] I think that Adams misses the fact that this moral sense is alive and relevant, but only for the author-equivalent characters and those the author-equivalent loves. In *Pale Fire,* Adams' immediate reference, the esthetic and moral senses are largely restricted to Shade's feelings and his poem, while the entire Gradus movement is set free to make its dismal hilarity and blood-spattered comedy out of anything and everything available, regardless of any system of values even remotely humane or rationally conceived. Gradus is an even lower evolutionary form than the Paduk we visualized in his "neglected aquarium" and confirms Nabokov's typical vision of evil as imbecile and subhuman:

[Gradus] could read, write and reckon, he was endowed with a modicum of self-awareness (with which he did not know what to do), some duration consciousness, and a good memory for faces. . . . Spiritually he did not exist. Morally he was a dummy pursuing another dummy. The fact that his weapon was a real one, and his quarry a highly developed human being, this fact belonged to *our* world of events. . . . Our Lord has fashioned man so marvelously that no amount of motive hunting and rational inquiry can ever *really* explain how and why anybody is capable of destroying a fellow creature. [278–279]

As with the Ekwilists, the monstrosity in Gradus is not any aspect of passion or revenge; it is simply a matter of "having been given an important, responsible assignment (which happened to require that he should kill) by a group of people sharing his notion of justice" (279). He has no sense of proportion. And again, the wisdom is collective, the motive power largely bureaucratic momentum. The "moral and humane dimensions" are quite powerfully present in Nabokov, but they do not extend to the Paduks and Graduses of the Nabokovian world. These brutes are the fit inheritors of the dynamic social philosophies of the twentieth century which can always tell us "what to do" with that oppressive, promising, puzzling self-consciousness we are afflicted with as human beings. The others, the Padukians and the good burghers, have long ago unburdened themselves of consciousness and followed the bracing advice that comes out of the State radios, one of which we conveniently overhear with Krug at a grocery store:

"From now on," continued the tremendously swollen Tyrannosaurus, "the way to total joy lies open. You will attain it, brothers, by dint of ardent intercourse with one another, by being like happy boys in a whispering dormitory, by adjusting ideas and emotions to those of a harmonious majority . . . dissolve in the virile oneness of the State. . . . Your groping individualities will become interchangeable and, instead of crouching in the prison cell of an illegal ego, the naked soul will be in contact with that of every other man in this land . . . each of you will be able to make his abode in the elastic inner self of any other citizen, and to flutter from one to another, until you know not whether you are Peter or John, so closely locked will you be in the embrace of the State. [85–86]

Besides containing suggestions of the Padukian homosexuality —the homophile is always a monster in Nabokov—this electronic cajoling is more or less an overt Nabokovian analysis of the hallucinations necessary to communism and Nazism. It is, of course, unthinkable for Krug to consider lowering himself into this tepid and dirty liquidity. The extreme sense of individuality in Nabokov's favorite characters is more than the reflex of an esthete or the hauteur of a snob (although those are real enough feelings and part of any true description of his sensibility). For Nabokov and his favorites, excellence is inconceivable for the collective, and the first condition of genius is isolation.

Recurrence

Few things are more useful to the reader of Nabokov than an awareness that his is the art of recurrence. Recurrence unifies and brings order. It is Nabokov's means of signaling to the reader, and it is also his means of signaling to the characters. Recurrence crystallizes from out of the random details of the narrative the pattern of little clues and codes that indicates the presence of its creator, the "mind behind the mirror." But let a cautionary qualification be added: some of the recurrent themes, events, ideas, or details are important only because of their recurrence and have no inherent significance. Olga appears again and again to her widower Krug, and her reappearance is emotionally significant for both Krug and the reader; the "spatulate" forms of liquid that recur again and again to signify to Krug and to us that he is, indeed, "in good hands" are important for their simultaneous extension into and out of the fictional plane, and they contribute a unique and fundamental set of meanings to the art. But "that which recurs" can frequently be minor and extraneous in Nabokov's work, and this fact should lead us to be skeptical about the relative weight and value of this or that motif. Although recurrence cannot easily be overemphasized as a significant aspect of Nabokov's technique, the motif itself, magnified in importance simply by the finder's thrill, must be judged in the context of the coherent esthetic and moral world that Nabokov creates for us to share. It is a coded message, not an end in itself.

Nabokov uses recurrence as the key technique in presenting the two women in Krug's life, Olga and Mariette. Olga Krug is wise, generous, vivacious, healthy, intelligent—the Ideal Faculty Wife to be set against Mariette's Dark Lady. Her image recurs six times in the course of Krug's dreaming in chapter 5, where his vision is of her taking off her jewelry after a ball. The image of Olga that gradually emerges from the oblique incidental and incremental details becomes at last an image of death and dissolution:

The two teachers pulled the curtains apart. Olga was revealed sitting before her mirror and taking off her jewels after the ball. Still clad in cherry-red velvet, her strong gleaming elbows thrown back and lifted like wings, she had begun to unclasp at the back of her neck her dazzling dog collar. He knew it would come off together with her vertebrae—that in fact it was the crystal of her vertebrae—and he experienced an agonizing sense of impropriety at the thought that everybody in the room would observe and take down in writing her inevitable, pitiful, innocent disintegration. [72]

The "teachers" in the first sentence are dream functionaries, but they are linked to the "lesson" of which Olga was the mannekin: "The theme to be tackled was an afternoon with Mallarmé . . . but the only part [Krug] could remember seemed to be *'le sanglot dont j'étais encore ivre'* " (71). Nabokov informs us in the Introduction that this fragment of a line is from *L'Après-Midi d'un Faune* and is thematically relevant because the full line, in which the faun accuses the nymph of disengaging herself from his embrace prematurely ("spurning the spasm with which I still was drunk"), suggests Krug's sexual excitement and ultimate frustration with Mariette, the spy-housekeeper, whose perfume is called *Sanglot* and whom he was on the point of sexually possessing when Mac, Linda, and the adolescent goons assigned to abduct David arrive and set off the last and most terrible of the novel's motions.

The contrast young Mariette makes with the vital and mature Olga is, of course, pronounced. Her sexuality is *sans merci,* her role the darker of the two primary Nabokovian female types. She is "Cinderella, the little slattern, moving and dusting in a dream, always ivory pale and unspeakably tired after last night's ball" (123). This Cinderella "micro-motif" tags along with her in an elaborate and private fashion, a code linking her to the kingdom of fairytale.

Pnin enunciates a famous etymological boner when he discusses the French *vair* in reference to Cinderella's slippers: they "were not made of glass but of Russian squirrel fur—*vair* in French . . . which . . . came not from *varius,* variegated, but from *veveritsa,* Slavic for a certain pale, winter-squirrel fur." (158). Therefore we should not be surprised to find that, among the collection of footgear offered to Krug at Paduk's HQ, is "a girl's tiny slipper trimmed with moth-eaten squirrel fur" (125), or that Krug hears at home "the sloppy tread of [Mariette's] old bed slippers trimmed with dirty fur" (141). She is directly referred to as Cinderella and is supposed to be both sweeping the floor and losing her slipper when he finds her in David's bedroom: "She had interupted her labors to pick up one of David's animal books and was now engrossed in it, half-sitting, half-lying athwart the bed, with one leg stretched far out, the bare ankle resting on the back of a chair, the slipper off, the toes moving," and Krug, afflicted with his own impersonal virility, averts "his eyes from the brownish-pink shadows she showed" (142). This minor theme recurs during the crucial scene of David's abduction, where her queer, adolescent sexuality also stirs Mac:

"I don't weigh much, you know," said Mariette, raising her elbows towards Mac. Blushing furiously, the young policeman cupped a perspiring paw under the girl's grateful thighs, put another around her ribs and lightly lifted her heavenwards. One of her slippers fell off.

"It's O.K.," she said quickly, "I can put my foot into your pocket. There. Lin will carry my slipper." [182]

A moment later sister Linda brings two key words into conjunction: "Here's your slipper and your fur" (183). And Mac himself finally, mysteriously finds access to the mysterious little motif:

"Sure you're not cold, Cin?"

His baritone voice was loaded with love. The teenager blushed and furtively pressed his hand. She said she was warm, oh, very warm. Feel for yourself. She blushed because he had employed a secret diminutive which none knew, which he had somehow divined. Intuition is the sesame of love. [186]

Although Nabokov informs us in the Introduction that all his books should be stamped "Freudians, Keep Out" (xviii), and Krug observes a situational reminder of his creator's attitude toward the "Viennese Quack" ("At the bottom of the [toilet] bowl a safety razor blade envelope with Dr. S. Freud's face and signature floated" [75]), the choice of the Cinderella micro-motif is apparently an aspect of Nabokov's own erotic sense, and since the fairytale itself does not fit Mariette very well, any metaphoric explanation of this motif would seem to be forced.

A very slender motif is repeated with much subtlety, and we

can infer that the author has taken great care in its delicate disguising. That care is the point, for the motif itself has no real allusive function: Mariette is not a *victim*, like Cinderella, and if she is one of three sisters, and the one who is serving as chambermaid, she is not mistaken for a grand lady by a prince, she has nothing that might be called a pumpkin-coach, and does not triumph in love at a ball.

The metamorphosis and interplay of these minor, easily overlooked recurrent details can be regarded as an authorial signature. A few other micro-motifs in *Bend Sinister* are the Bervok apples, which appear and reappear; Dr. Alexander's pet phrase, "The ugliest wives are the truest"; the appearances of the rebel leader Phokus; and, for a good sample of meticulous irrelevancy and wholly private significance, a twenty-four-instrument penknife that we first see on the tray of confiscated weapons in the Institute film and that later turns up in the hands of Crystalsen, the master goon, while the overvoice deadpans a description of him "cleaning his nails with a steel shoe-buttoner contained, together with twenty-three other instruments, in a fat pocketknife which he had filched somewhere during the day" (206). The knife reappears again immediately ("Crystalsen's firm fingernails getting at one twenty-fourth of the tight penknife" [207]). Even more curiously and privately, the key number, twenty-four, seems to breed its own importance when Paduk, disguised as a cellmate, tries once more to get Krug to endorse his fantastic and vile regime. Notice the recurrence of the numbers:

"Listen, Gurdamak. We are going to make you a last offer. Four friends you had, four staunch friends and true. Deep in a dungeon they languish and moan. Listen, Drug, listen Kamerad, I am ready to give them and some twenty other *liberalishki* their freedom, if you agree to what you had practically agreed to yesterday. Such a small thing! The lives of twenty-four men are in your hands. . . .

Think, what marvellous power! You sign your name and twenty-two men and two women flock out into the sunlight. It is your last chance. Madamka, say yes!"

"Go to hell, you filthy Toad," said Krug wearily. [208]

Nabokov, who controls coincidence as well as everything else in the novel, is demonstrating his presence within it through his use of recurrence, coincidence, and iteration, and thus the value is not intrinsic. Alfred Appel itemizes dozens of references to Clare Quilty aside from his onstage presence in *Lolita,* and shows us the numerous references linking that tale of love and death to Poe's "Annabel Lee." A great many odds and ends recur within novels or from novel to novel. Here I have exhaustively insisted upon the micro-motifs in this Exhibit A manner, but the cardinal point is quite important, and the temptation, for academic types, quite seductive: recurrence and correspondence and coincidence in Nabokov's work should be viewed as an important but not entirely accessible system of coherence, far more useful to Nabokov than it is to us. It should never be allowed to distract us from the evaluation and enjoyment of the fiction of which it is but a minor part. To concentrate on the elaboration of the micro-motifs, a quantitative phenomenon and a statistical aggregate, is to miss the significance of Nabokov's creative act—an act whose mysteriousness he himself constantly reaffirms. Nabokov's creations are always aware of their own miraculousness and always calling attention to their creator. It is as if the deity not only creates the local rocks, but creates them complete with sophisticated graffiti, private codes, obscure initials already carved into them.

Perhaps the best explanation of Nabokov's use of recurrence is to point out that, narrative being inherently a linear process and Nabokovian narrative being at least partially a problem-solving activity—a "clash" conducted between the creator and the reader through the medium of the characters—recurrence is the most fitting means of introducing, and then revealing, the presence, intentions, and interests of that deity.

In *Speak, Memory,* Nabokov, citing nature's example, talks about his own feelings and predilections as artist; notice that nature's "miraculous coincidence"—too much coincidence—becomes what he calls a "new truth." Further, this new truth in its "subtlety, exuberance, and luxury" exists for no practical purpose. The mystery behind things, here personified as "Nature," has its own mysterious reasons. It behaves, in fact, like an artist.

The mysteries of mimicry had a special attraction for me. Its phenomena showed an artistic perfection usually associated with man-wrought things. . . . When a certain moth resembles a certain wasp in shape and color, it also walks and moves its antennae in a waspish, unmothlike manner. When a butterfly has to look like a leaf, not only are all the details of a leaf beautifully rendered but markings mimicking grub-bored holes are generously thrown in. "Natural selection," in the Darwinian sense, could not explain the miraculous coincidence of imitative aspect and imitative behavior, nor could one appeal to the theory of the "struggle for life" when a protective device was carried to the point of mimetic subtlety, exuberance, and luxury far in excess of a predator's power of appreciation. I discovered in nature the nonutilitarian delights that I sought in art. Both were a form of magic, both were a game of intricate enchantment and deception.[8]

Recurrence of detail in a linear, cumulative art such as narration is the most useful means by which the local god, whose glory is to hide a thing, can conceal that thing in such a way that the reader can gradually discover its presence. This is the way in which the "mind behind the mirror" reveals himself. It is the narrative artist's best means of imitating the esthetic intentions we should perceive in the natural world. It is art imitating an artful nature. But it should always be remembered that the hidden thing itself may or may not be intrinsically important.

Time and Death

The most important use of recurrence in *Bend Sinister* is to make the reader aware of planes of artifice above the plane on which the fictional characters exist. We are deliberately exposed to glimpses of the creator's ink-stained thumb and forefinger, a throbbing puppet string the concealment of which is purposely imperfect, the sudden self-consciousness of the rhetorical over-voice and, ultimately, Nabokov's materialization on the page itself as Krug is destroyed by the Ekwilist police:

[Krug] saw the Toad crouching at the foot of the wall, shaking, dissolving, speeding up his shrill incantations, protecting his dimming face with his transparent arm, and Krug ran towards him and just a fraction of an instant before another and better bullet hit him, he shouted again: You, you—and the wall vanished, like a rapidly withdrawn slide, and I stretched myself and got up from among the chaos of written and rewritten pages, to investigate the sudden twang that something had made in striking the wire netting of my window.

As I had thought, a big moth was clinging with furry feet to the netting, on the night's side . . . then it let go and swung back into the warm damp darkness.

. . . I knew that the immortality I had conferred on [Krug] was a slippery sophism, a play upon words. But the very last lap of his life had been happy and it had been proven to him that death was but a question of style . . .

Across the lane . . . I could also distinguish the glint of a special puddle (the one Krug had somehow perceived through the layer of his own life), an oblong puddle invariably acquiring the same form after every shower because of the constant spatulate shape of a depression in the ground. Possibly, something of the kind may be said to occur in regard to the imprint we leave in the intimate texture of space. [216–217]

Notice that at the end, Paduk is "dissolving" and "transparent." The dissolution of that monstrous but absurd world of terror and torture occurs at the climax of *Invitation to a Beheading* as well. Cincinnatus is saved by "beings akin to him," while the bestial world that wanted to behead him for the crime of being "opaque"—Nabokov's code for all in us that is private, real, mysterious, unique—reduces itself to a collapsing stage-set of "flapping scenery."

One hesitates to try to yoke a complete discursive explanation to Nabokov's theme in these important instances. There is, demonstrably, the undercurrent of outrage that always overtakes Nabokov when he is dealing with Marx, Freud, the Third Reich, or the Communists. There is, possibly, the feeling that the bestial worlds collapse because they have purposely extinguished "the only real thing in the world," human consciousness, and like the Etermon cartoon figures, they contain nothing worthy or capable of "transcending mortality." But the full effect on the reader which these endings provide is not so easily analyzed.

Nabokov claims a triumph in what he calls, in the Introduction, "Krug's blessed madness when he suddenly perceives the simple reality of things and knows but cannot express in the words of his world that he and his son and his wife and everybody else are merely my whims and megrims" (xiv). This statement obviously calls attention to the curious motives which move one man to create a fiction and other men to read and "believe" in it.

It is perhaps surprising for an author to point out that the characters on the flimsy scrim of his narrative are imaginary creations whose only vitality is derived from the belief in them which he and the reader share. But what the author points out is not really a shock to our skeptical sense, which is as indispensable as the suspension of disbelief, and which always reminds us that the distinction between the art we are witnessing and the life it imitates is not relative but absolute. No matter how thin and transparent the membrane between art and life becomes—and art's charm and power are in part gauged by terms like "realistic" and "convincing," which are tributes to the thinness and transparency of the membrane—the distinction between them is pure, absolutely denying life to the world of art. If we cannot agree upon a positive definition of art, we can still perhaps agree that it is the antithesis of life; and if we insist, as I think we must and should, on using terms which attribute that which is lifelike to art when we describe it, we must remember that art is a mirror-world. The "life" a work of art can be said to reflect cannot really be life at all, for art surrenders the essential possibilities of life—its effect on our world and its ability to change—and this surrender seems to enable us not only to suspend disbelief but to maintain it, for disbelief is the one sense life never allows us, it is the one sense reserved wholly for art.

Put in other terms, art allows the participant a skepticism which life does not, and this skepticism seems a necessary part of the esthetic reaction. The destruction of Krug and his son is painful to the reader, it is esthetically and morally terrible; perhaps more powerfully than any other story it evokes Auschwitz. But it is imaginary. It is not life, although it imitates life with wrenching accuracy. However terrible its progression, the participants are not real and never were; and I think most of us would agree that a minor accident to someone we love in this world generates in us an emotion that is not only more intense but seems to be, as far as we can tell about these things, different in *kind* from the emotions generated out of *Bend Sinister* or any other work of art. Is not an important part of the attractions of "order" that art is always claimed to provide its absolute powerlessness, changelessness, and finitude? Isn't the pleasure of the tragic story dependent upon the relentless and continuous denial that what we watch is real?

Nabokov's penetration into the novel can only modify the feelings that have been generated out of the story. The author, in calling attention to himself and his work, is really engaging in a redundancy, for we have been aware of the creator all along—we always are.

> In the middle of the night something in a dream shook [Krug] out of his sleep into what was really a prison cell with bars of light (and a separate pale gleam like the footprint of some phosphorescent islander) breaking the darkness . . . the luminous pattern he saw assumed a strange, perhaps fatal significance, the key to which was half-hidden by a flap of dark consciousness on the glimmering floor of a half-remembered nightmare. It would seem that some promise had been broken, some design thwarted, some opportunity missed—or so grossly exploited as to leave an afterglow of sin and shame. The pattern of light was somehow the result of a kind of stealthy, abstractly vindictive, groping, tampering movement that had been going on in a dream, or behind a dream, in a tangle of immemorial and by now formless and aimless machinations. Imagine a sign that warns you of an explosion in such cryptic or childish language that you wonder whether everything . . . has not been reproduced artificially . . . by special arrangement with the mind behind the mirror. [209]

Grossness, broken promises, exploitation, "sin," "shame," "vindictive," "formless," "aimless," the "pang of pity" are terms that Nabokov uses when he describes his own role, and they are honest terms. By taking responsibility for Krug's tale, Nabokov admits he is responsible for creating a hideous fiction of blood and terror and torture and monstrous, unredeemed suffering. The fact that he has plagiarized it from life, from twentieth-century history, does not excuse its existence. Evidently the deity had other reasons for telling the tale in addition to the cruelty, grossness, and opportunism that he by implication attributes to himself, but what those reasons were is a question he does not pose and one I would guess he would not like to answer. We learn from the Introduction that the tale was "written and should be read" to the accompaniment of Krug's heartbeats, but an explanation of the savagery of the tale is nowhere to be found. If Krug "understands he is in good hands" during his "moonburst of madness," the infinitely more troubling question of why he was first abandoned to such bad hands is never either posed or answered.

The Part and the Whole

Nabokov will always sacrifice the whole for the part. This statement, although overly dramatic, does describe an aspect of his practice. Nabokov's fiction almost always ignores the possibilities of subordination in favor of the possibilities of inclusion and magnification.

In his brilliant analysis of *Lolita,* Martin Green, describing Humbert-as-narrator, mentions Tolstoy: "This narrator is clearly someone both master and servant of his own taste for brilliant language. Anything vivid enough to demand to be said he will say, and retrieve his sincerity later—will temporarily throw away his identity and his serious purposes for an effect. . . . There is a wealth of literary and linguistic reference, indulged in partly for its own sake, and as a game. . . . These are personal displays of cleverness on the writer's part; [and they] *are* what Tolstoy called the marks of bad art."[9]

Nabokov's intentions and those of Tolstoy are, of course, almost completely antithetical. Nabokov, in his role of reptilian esthete, can proclaim in an interview that "a work of art has no importance whatever to society. It is only important to the individual, and only the individual reader is important to me. I don't give a damn for the group, the community, the masses, and so forth."[10] Tolstoy, however, in what Nabokov described as his "hyperethical stage," rejects the decadent art of the esthete for the regenerated art of the imminent future, when "only those productions will be esteemed art which transmit feelings drawing men together in brotherly union, or such universal feelings as can unite all men."[11]

Events have given to Tolstoy's statement an irony he did not intend: it has become almost an epigraph for the buoyant Russian liberal optimism that helped to hatch one of mankind's most terrible tyrannies. The same events and subsequent ones seem to justify Nabokov's profound skepticism about the extraliterary benefits of literature. Nabokov's art is moral and contains wholesome relationships and a consistent vision of good and evil within the individual and even within a society, but these aspects of his work are confined to the author-equivalent and the favorite characters, and are not at all the norms of the world that surrounds them. As we shall see, the problem of "evil" in *Lolita* is complex, but the novel is, in fact, organized with deep and sensitive attention to moral imperatives, and its vision is comprehensive, humane, and wholesome. The moral life of Nabokov's characters typically shows no development at all. A simple and terrible opposition exists between the isolated individual human consciousness and the bestial and lobotomized State, and neither changes its characteristics or possibilities in the slightest.

Nabokov's fiction frequently contains extraneous matter created and kept for its own sake. Nabokov refuses to limit fiction to the interaction and careers of a group of characters confined to one narrative plane. He almost always includes sources of interest and amusement that are quasi-narrative or extranarrative, and in *Bend Sinister* he arranges for an elaborate disgression on *Hamlet*.

Frank Kermode writes that the *Hamlet* disgression is a "useless but agreeable exercise of intellect and will contrasting with the smooth bestiality of the police."[12] The passage deals with a conversation between Ember, in bed in his room, translating Shakespeare into the local Russo-Teutonic language in his capacity as the new Literary Advisor to the State Theatre; and Krug, haunted but not paralyzed by his widowerhood. The *Hamlet* of which they speak is twofold. It is the marvelous *Hamlet* they visualize in their mind's eye and, in ugly and funny contrast to this vision, it is also Professor Hamm's "The Real Plot of *Hamlet*," which begins:

" 'In *Hamlet* the exposition grimly promises the audience a play founded upon young Fortinbras' attempt to recover the lands lost by his father to King Hamlet. This is the conflict, this is the plot. To surreptitiously shift the stress from this healthy, vigorous and clear-cut Nordic theme to the chameleonic moods of an impotent Dane would be, on the modern stage, an insult to determinism and common sense . . . popular common sense must spit out the caviar of moonshine and poetry, and the simple word, *verbum sine ornatu*, intelligible to man and beast alike, and accompanied by fit action, must be restored to power.' " [96–97]

The Hamm thesis, too juicy for Nabokov to merely dismiss, elaborates itself into a grotesquery of Ekwilist inanities, complete with old Fortinbras' ghost substituting for that of Hamlet père ("The ghost of the victim posing as the ghost of the murdered— what a wonderful bit of farseeing strategy, how deeply it excites our intense admiration!") and with anti-Semitic overtones of Nazi-Communist pronouncements as in "some masonic maneuver engendered by the Shylocks of high finance" (97).

Ember finishes a long passage of parody with an oblique apology from his digressing creator: "Well, this gives you a fair sample of what I have to endure." Important information is then exchanged—Ember had overseen Olga's cremation, Krug and David had gone to the country where their stay with the Maximovs had been interrupted by the arrest of the old couple—but Nabokov whirls through this in a paragraph in order to get back to *Hamlet:* "In order to bring things back to a less emotional level Krug tells [Ember] about a curious character with whom he once traveled in the States, a man who was fanatically eager to make a film out of *Hamlet*" (99). One suspects that Nabokov himself is the one who is eager for the scenario, for it is presented in elaborate detail and consumes the next six pages of the novel.

Critics have in general tried to prove the organic relationship between the *Hamlet* digression and the rest of the novel. One critic begins with the reassurance that "there are admittedly times when Nabokov indulges himself, but the longest of the digressions, the Shakespearean one, is not only functional, but an absolutely necessary part of the novel—it is an assertion of the value of literature. And one element of literature is the sheer joy of seeing words used intelligently and sensitively."[13]

This statement is unconvincing in several ways. First, the critic does not make clear to whom Nabokov is supposed to be asserting the "value of literature," whether to the characters or the reader. In which group is this "sheer joy" aroused? Are the joy-arousing possibilities of using words "intelligently and sensitively" confined to parallel, extranarrative passages like the *Hamlet* digression? Finally, this assertion of "value" in literature disagrees with Nabokov's own esthetic tenets; notice that the following statements all resist the assignment of any exterior value or function to a work of art:

Fancy is fertile only when it is futile.[14]

A writer is lost when he grows interested in such questions as "What is Art?" and "What is the artist's duty?"[15]

. . . all great literary achievements [are] a phenomenon of language and not of ideas.[16]

I discovered in nature the nonutilitarian delights that I sought in art.[17]

Gogol at his best, that is, using his imagination for the purpose of a complex and unnecessary deception . . .[18]

At this superhigh level of art, literature is of course not concerned with pitying the underdog, or cursing the upper-dog. It appeals to that secret depth of the human soul where the shadows of other worlds pass like the shadows of nameless and soundless ships . . . this is really the only appeal that interests me.[19]

A work of art has no importance to society.[20]

My books are not only blessed by a total lack of social significance, but are also mythproof: Freudians flutter around them avidly, approach with itching oviducts, stop, sniff, and recoil.[21]

Every statement of Nabokov's and every aspect of his work should convince critics of the danger in assigning "value" of various kinds to his work or demonstrating "organic" connections between planes, scenes, characters, voices, themes, and motifs in his fiction. In the critical passage quoted above only the phrase "sheer joy" can be redeemed: it describes the sense of exhilaration always marked in Nabokov's best work, and the critic should not have tried to join its wonderful, obvious, and *important* narcissism with some sort of "value," perhaps for Krug or perhaps the reader.

No intelligent reader of Nabokov should be content with the false satisfactions of discovering tenuous parallels. His art is much more subtle than its most recondite "wayside murmur," for it includes within itself a recognition—half awe, half irritation—of the irreducibility and self-sufficiency and ineffability of the artistic process. Nabokov refuses to obligate himself to any system of coherence, internal or external, which circumscribes the imagination or tries to impose a misleading sense of order on the mysteries it can only reflect: "We shall never know the origin of life, or the meaning of life, or the nature of space and time, or the nature of nature, or the nature of thought."[22]

This sense of the unattainability of some kinds of "knowledge" receives implied or explicit formulation everywhere in Nabokov; it should warn the reader to accept no easy interpretations. Nabokov states, quite truly, quite passionately, that "art is never simple . . . [that claim is] a vulgar absurdity. Art at its greatest is fantastically deceitful and complex."[23] But if art exists only for its own sake, even when it is at the same time the most beautiful and irresistible impulse of which human consciousness is capable, it is also powerless to help us. Nabokov recognizes this acutely, and a sense of existential dismay and cheerful nihilism is powerful in his favorite characters. For example, when Krug looks at his own philosophical accomplishments, all he can perceive is intriguing destruction and ultimate futility: "He had delicately taken apart the systems of others and had acquired thereby a reputation for an impish sense of humour and delightful common sense whereas in fact he was a big sad hog of a man and the 'common-sense' affair had turned out to be the gradual digging of a pit to accommodate pure smiling madness" (153).

Thought or art can put on a dazzling show, but the laws of time and death are as inexorable, and esthetically as banal, as the law of gravity; Krug's thought is no different. No thought can be. Note the underlying tension in the extended image of thought-as-aging-acrobat in the following passage, which describes the spangles on a woman's wrap: "Those mirrors of infinite space . . . where Olga is not, but where mythology stretches strong circus nets, lest thought, in its ill-fitting tights, should break its old neck instead of rebouncing with a hep and a hop . . . [as he] catches the little blue handkerchief, which his musclar flying mate, after her own exertions, takes from her heaving hot bosom —heaving more than her smile suggests—and tosses to him, so that he may wipe the palms of his aching weakening hands" (54)'.

The difference between art and life, or thought and life, is absolute, and one should remember that, after the world of the fictional characters in *Bend Sinister* has been assumed into the "bosom of its maker," Nabokov confesses that "I knew that the immortality that I had conferred on [Krug] was [only] a slippery sophism, a play upon words" (217).

No matter what powers are exerted in creating it, art must remain art—unliving, finite, powerless. The "big moth" that clings to Nabokov's windowscreen "on the night side" in the book's final sentences is, he informs us in the Introduction, "Olga's rosy soul" (xviii), but the apparent fragility of that screen separating soul from creator is only a delicious illusion: it is as strong as time and death. Art is, after all, only an illusion; consciousness is, after all, no more durable than the "aching and weakening" body it inhabits, and neither Nabokov nor his equivalents ever ignore this. Part of the poignancy of *Lolita* arises from our recognition that we are reading a posthumous work. As Humbert Humbert tells us in the last two paragraphs of the novel, he has realized that he cannot "parade living Lolita" before a judge and jury to save himself, and I think that here we should feel Nabokov is dismissing the mock-confessional motives of Humbert's memoir in favor of wholly esthetic ones:

And do not pity C. Q. [Clare Quilty]. One had to choose between him and H. H., and one wanted H. H. to exist at least a couple of months longer, so as to have him make you live in the minds of later generations. I am thinking of aurochs and angels, the secret of durable pigments, prophetic sonnets, the refuge of art. And this is the only immortality you and I may share, my Lolita. [311]

Here, as everywhere in Nabokov's worlds, art is fascinating and futile; time and death, brutal and banal and yet triumphant.

2

Nabokov's
Short Fiction

"Cloud, Castle, Lake"

Just as in *Bend Sinister,* the conflict between the individual
and the group, and the enormous disparity between these con-
tenders are a constant concern in Nabokov's short fiction, and
there is again little ambiguity about what is of value in the conflict or which side we should choose (the weaker—in Nabokov,
a lobotomy is a sign of strength). Just as in the novels, a unique
and mercurial strain in the short fiction derives from a variant
of the romantic vision: Nabokov insists that there is a mystery
behind things, and what we are accustomed to call real life is but
a stage set quickly patched together out of the simplest, cheapest
odds and ends, such as chlorophyll, carbon, and the law of gravity. Speaking with heartfelt irony in *Despair,* Hermann claims
"the nonexistence of God is easy to prove . . . [for how could
he] employ his time in such inane fashion as playing with man-
nikins [and] . . . restrict his game to the dreadfully trite laws of
mechanics, chemistry, and mathematics."[1] Behind this stage set
looms something that may be either "blissful" or "terrible" but
is surely miraculous. God, Fate, and Art are various terms for it,
and the problem is endlessly suggestive for Nabokov. And just
as in the longer fiction, the commonsensical middleground of
manners, money, minor epiphany, life mimicked or sliced, insti-

tutions, social ambition, and so on is almost wholly ignored. And here again the difference between art and life—or fantasy and life—is one of the story's main concerns and part of its complex of meaning.

A story called "Cloud, Castle, Lake" is illustrative. The plot is spare. The narrator reports that one of his literary representatives, "a modest, mild bachelor, very efficient," happens to win a pleasure trip at a charity ball given in Berlin for Russian émigrés. "[Vasili] did not care to go anywhere, but when he tried to sell his ticket at the office of the Bureau of Pleasantrips he was told that to do so he would have to have special permission from the Ministry of Transportation; when he tried them, it turned out that first he would have to draw up a complicated petition at a notary's on stamped paper; and besides, a so-called 'certificate of non-absence from the city for the summertime' had to be obtained from the police. . . . So he sighed a little, and decided to go" (99).

The opposition of the isolated and rational human consciousness and the monstrous and prolific bureaucratic organism which has substituted blue ink, notary seals, and stamped paper for that consciousness is, of course, a primary Nabokovian antithesis. Nabokov demonstrates his favoritism in regard to Vasili not only by the direct use of quiet praise, but by such muted suggestions as a mention that the émigré ball is a *charity* affair, a mention which substitutes a humanitarian motive for a social one in his protagonist. A Nabokovian favorite would never try to lose his loneliness in a crowd, especially not in an organized crowd. The author goes on to describe Vasili as a "likeable little man . . . his eyes so intelligent and kind." When Nabokov shows evidence of really liking his protagonist, the reader should realize that disaster can't be far away.

Vasili buys some camping equipment in preparation for the

trip, and the night before his departure by train he dreams that "this trip, thrust upon him by a feminine Fate in a low-cut gown, this trip which he had accepted so reluctantly, would bring him some wonderful, tremulous happiness." Notice that the personification of Fate being seductive is more than a bit of comic opportunism; everywhere in Nabokov's work the term "Fate" represents that mystery or Mystery behind the phenomenological world, and this mystery expresses itself in discernible signals, coincidences, and combinations.

Vasili finds himself in an "unmistakably third-class" coach of a train, complete with an enormous and muscular guide in Tyrolese garb (doubtless a relative of Mac in *Bend Sinister*), two male Shultzes and "two fidgety women with big mouths and big rumps," a red-headed widow, and "a dark young man by the name of Schramm, with lustreless eyes and a vague velvety vileness about his person" who, like Dr. Alexander in *Bend Sinister,* turns out to be in disguise: Schramm is a sort of *agent provocateur* for the Bureau of Pleasantrips, whose job is to make sure that everyone thoroughly enjoys himself.

Vasili, deprived of his volume of Tyutchev by the group, tries to enjoy the beautiful summer morning as seen from the swift train: "What charm the world acquires when it is wound up and moving like a merry-go-round!" Quite soon the scenery acquires for him a magic that is both nostalgic and promising, "a memory of love, disguised as a meadow." The social organism that has surrounded Vasili but not yet digested him grows more powerful as the journey progresses. Sheet music is passed around, and the communal jollity becomes vocal:

> In a paradise of heather
> Where the field mouse screams and dies
> Let us march and sweat together
> With the steel-and-leather guys!   [103]

As night overtakes the train, the group that surrounds Vasili becomes a Boschian collective, a "wobbly, many-handed being, from which one could not escape," and the next day's hike is equally loathsome and humiliating. Vasili is continually forced into witless games, none of which he can play well. "He was acknowledged the loser and was forced to eat a cigarette butt."

Suddenly, on the second day's hike, exhausted and even physically threatened by the sinister group, Vasili comes upon a strange vision: cloud and castle, reflected in a nameless little lake. "Of course, there are plenty of such views in Central Europe, but just this one—in the inexpressible and unique harmoniousness of its three principal parts, in its smile, in some mysterious innocence it had, my love! my obedient one!—was something so unique, and so familiar, and so long-promised, and it so *understood* the beholder that Vasili Ivanovich even pressed his hand to his heart, as if to see if his heart was still there in order to give it away" (105).

Stealing off to an inn on the edge of the lake, Vasili finds a room with this view, and "in one radiant second" realizes that "in this little room with that view, beautiful to the verge of tears, life would at last be what he had always wished it to be." But on returning to the group to tell them that he intends to stay forever, Vasili touches off the communal instinct that enforces total conformity, that denies the impulse of the sensitive consciousness to isolate itself in a world Nabokov calls "other states of being . . . worlds of tenderness, brightness, and beauty," a Platonic super-world behind ours. " 'There can be no question of *anyone*—in this case you—refusing to continue this communal journey, . . . I am responsible for each of you, and shall bring back each of you, alive or dead,' " the leader tells him, and Vasili is "swept along a forest road as in a hideous fairy tale . . . the radiance behind his back receded, fractured by trees, and then it was no longer there." Besides being removed from the source of his happiness, Vasili is beaten so severely Paduk himself might have been almost satisfied.

On one level, the story is Nabokov's essential social parable. The relationship between the group and the torture is almost syllogistically simple, a universal law of communal behavior. There can be no interaction between the individual and the group except on a grossly destructive level; the possibilities that either of them will learn and change are simply nonexistent.

The fairytale atmosphere of the story is not only a matter of setting and simplified oppositions, it resides also in the miraculousness of Vasili's discovery—or his recovery, for the revelation of cloud, castle, and lake is Platonic; the vision seems to have existed before, in a dimension that now penetrates into Vasili's and that he seems to recognize from prior knowledge or intuition.

The similarity in thematic scheme of this story and *Bend Sinister* need hardly be insisted upon; even the narrator—the story is told in a very elastic version of first-person narration—assumes an oblique deification, for in the last paragraph Vasili returns to the narrator, presents his sad tale, and we are told he "begged me to let him go, insisted that he could not continue, that he had not the strength to belong to mankind any longer. Of course," the narrator tells us, "I let him go."

Nabokov told Andrew Field that Vasili will not go back to the lake: " 'He will never find it again. If I let him go, it is in the hope that he might find a less dangerous job than that of my agent.' "[2] Once again, Nabokov shows his sympathetic concern for his creation and the importance of the linkage between writer and created character. Nabokov's art is almost always extremely partisan, visible, intrusive, and consciously artifical. In *Despair,* Nabokov chooses to reveal Hermann to the police by having them discover his link with Felix, the tramp he murders, through the clue of Felix's walking stick. Like all "good" clues, it has been shown to the reader several times in the course of the novel, and this flaunting of stick is the device that Hermann mocks: "With his stick, reader, with his stick. S-T-I-C-K, gentle reader. A roughly hewn stick branded with the owner's name: Felix Wohl-fahrt from Zwickau. With his stickau . . . gentle or lowly reader, with his stick! You know what a stick is, don't you?"[3]

Just as in the confrontation between Krug and Paduk, Nabo-kov chooses to retain and yet control a genre device. Here it is a clumsy "clue," which, by parodying, he controls. Parody is, among many other things, a way of having your cake and eating it, of retaining an effect while at the same time denying it full importance or approval. As we should expect, parody is especially useful to a self-conscious artist with no interest in naturalism and a great deal of interest in the "fireworks and tender sky" avail-able to the rhetorical overvoice. It allows pure and unrealistic forces to be juxtaposed with fairytale, melodramatic simplicity and still take on subtler tints of intelligence, irony, and discrim-ination. It is a means of qualification and, more important, of preservation. Nowhere in Nabokov are the sentiments beneath the surface ambiguous, and his moral world, unlike his protean means of presentation, is spare, clear, and primal.

"Spring in Fialta"

"Spring in Fialta" is a longer, more complex, and far more beautifully realized short story than "Cloud, Castle, Lake." Again, the plot is simple, if by plot we mean merely the events in the story.

The narrator, a Russian émigré businessman, finds himself in the midst of the evocative season and place of the story's title, having left his wife and children at home in Germany. Here in Fialta, "a lovely Crimean town," he meets again a Russian woman named Nina whom he has encountered over a period of years, several times sexually, but always for periods of only a few hours. Nina is accompanying the latest of her husbands, a repulsive Franco-Hungarian writer of genius named Ferdinand, and his friend Segur, who is just as repulsive but without genius. For an hour or so of warm and humid noonday penetrated by memories of irretrievably lost time, Victor, the narrator, walks and talks with these people. They leave him in Fialta just after he has made a futile, half-hearted overture to Nina: " 'Look here —what if I love you?' Nina glanced at me, I repeated those words, I wanted to add . . . but something like a bat passed swiftly across her face, a quick, queer, almost ugly expression . . . and our romance was even more hopeless than it had ever been."

The next day Victor discovers from the newspaper that the vehicle in which the trio were leaving town has crashed into the truck of a traveling circus: "Ferdinand and his friend, those invulnerable rogues, those salamanders of fate, those basilisks of good fortune, had escaped with local and temporary injury to their scales, while Nina, in spite of her long-standing, faithful imitation of them, had turned out after all to be mortal" (143).

All of Nabokov's art is multidimensional, constructed of different planes of the "real" and the "artificial." Not only is "Spring in Fialta" a series of superimposed transparencies, but the story of the characters on the narrative plane in itself embodies simultaneous but distinct themes. It should be remembered that Nabokov's prose and his vignettes, images, evocations, and metaphors exist for their own sake and are often more important than the skeletal events from which they are hung. In one sense, "fate" in Nabokov is a principle of pathetic fallacy that schemes and contrives behind the set of appearances and logical connections we call "reality"; in another sense, fate is one means of disguising the relatively arbitrary and inorganic connections between the scenes, paragraphs, images, and effects for which Nabokov sometimes finds a hastily constructed home that only seems to bear a real relationship to the rest of the work: the part is frequently more important than the whole. An analysis of his work must always take these factors into account at every step.

The most subtle distinction in the story seems to lie in its insistence on the difference between life and art, with Nina subtly representing life's mortality, and Ferdinand and Segur carrying suggestions of invulnerable but less valuable art. Nina becomes a victim of her own "long-standing, faithful imitation" of a kind of carelessness and invulnerability that can never be available to the real, but only to the artificial. This contrast is consistent throughout. Victor describes Ferdinand in terms that suggest the essential antithesis: "Having mastered the art of verbal invention to perfection, he particularly prided himself on being a weaver of words, a title he valued higher than that of writer; personally, I never could understand what was the good of thinking up books, of penning things that had not really happened in some way or other; and I remember once saying to him as I braved the mockery of his encouraging nods that, were I a writer, I should allow only my heart to have imagination, and for the rest rely upon memory, that long-drawn sunset shadow of one's personal truth" (130–131).

The pejorative connotation implied about things that "had not really happened in some way or other" and Victor's preference for memory, the preservation of the real, over imagination, the creation of the artificial, set up important contrasts with Ferdinand's heartless artificiality.

Segur, Ferdinand's companion, is described as "dapper, doll-like, rosy . . . a lover of art and a perfect fool" (134), and Ferdinand is the magnetic core of a salon of artistic fakers. Everywhere the opposition between these two forces, life and art, is subtle but consistent. Nina is not really Ferdinand's "fellow convict," although she imitakes his artificiality. It is important that she has no *direct* connection with art: "At the time we met, [Ferdinand's] *'Passage à niveau'* was being acclaimed in Paris; he was, as they say, 'surrounded,' and Nina (whose adaptability was an amazing substitute for the culture she lacked) had already assumed if not the part of a muse at least that of a soul mate and subtle adviser, following Ferdinand's creative convolutions and loyally sharing his artistic tastes; for although it is wildly improbable that she had ever waded through a single volume of his, she had a magic knack of gleaning all the best passages from the shop talk of his literary friends" (131).

Nina is not a "muse," she has no culture, she only "loyally" shares Ferdinand's tastes, she fakes an acquaintance with his work. But her imitation of Ferdinand's world is fatal to her, for Ferdinand is connected only with artificiality and death, art and antilife: "With every new book the tints [of Ferdinand's prose] grew still more dense, the gules and purpure still more ominous; and today one can no longer see anything at all through that blazoned, ghastly rich glass, and it seems that were one to break it, nothing but a perfectly black void would face one's shivering soul" (131).

It is that "black void" which ultimately defeats Nina's brave little show; Ferdinand is of that void; she is of something different, at once more vulnerable and more valuable.

In this story the narrator, Victor, must *not* be a writer, an artificer, or, as one critic calls him, a "sub-artist,"[4] because his judgment on Ferdinand and his alliance with Nina on the vital, vulnerable side of the membrane between life and art are necessary for the story's complex of feelings: "I grew apprehensive because something lovely, delicate, and unrepeatable was being wasted: something which I abused by snapping off poor bright bits in gross haste while neglecting the modest but true core which perhaps it kept offering me in a pitiful whisper. . . . Was there any practical chance of life together with Nina? . . . No, the thing was absurd. . . . Was she not chained to her husband by something stronger than love—the staunch friendship between two convicts?" (137–138).

The narrator's error here is to assume that Nina is made of the same stuff as Ferdinand, and Nina's error is to assume it, too. Life can only imitate art.

Nabokov has included in this story a curious self-incarnation; one hesitates to define it as symbolic, but it is at least a micro-motif suggestive of the creator's materialization and of Olga's transformation into the moth on the other side of the window-screen in *Bend Sinister*. Nabokov includes a "plus-foured Englishman of the solid exportable sort" in the opening description of Fialta. This Englishman soon appears again, licking his lips, and the narrator, following "the direction of his glance," sees Nina. The connection between creator and his character is thus subtly established. Just before Nina's death it is enlarged: "There was no one on the veranda where we lunched except the Englishman I had recently observed; in front of him, a long glass containing a bright crimson drink threw an oval reflection on the tablecloth. In his eyes, I noticed the same bloodshot desire, but now it was in no sense related to Nina; that avid look was not directed at her at all, but was fixed on the upper right-hand corner of the broad window near which he was sitting" (139).

The overtones of that "bright crimson drink" and the bloodshot desire" adumbrate the accident in an obvious way. In a moment the Englishman, the blood, and Ferdinand are connected: " 'I would like some of that pigeon's blood, too,' [Ferdinand] continued in the same loud, ripping voice, addressing the waiter, who understood his desire only after he had looked in the direction of the long-nailed finger which unceremoniously pointed at the Englishman's glass." This Englishman's last appearance is a prefiguration of Nina's "death," if by that death we also mean Olga's "death" and the reincarnation of her soul as a moth in the world of art. The Englishman, if we take him as a type of Nabokov himself, then represents the artist himself—the artist who creates and then reclaims his creation for esthetic reasons. "Meanwhile the big Englishman suddenly made up his mind, got up on a chair, stepped from there onto the window sill, and stretched up till he reached that coveted corner of the frame where rested a compact furry moth, which he deftly slipped into a pillbox" (141). After all, in a work of art, it is the artist himself who creates fate.

The adumbrations of Nina's death are everywhere in the story, and Victor's hindsight gives the story not only the enigmatic coherence of Nina's fate working itself out, obscurely but with perfect finality, but also allows him to draw an emotional if not logical connection between her personality and her destiny. Early in the story Victor tells us that he "cannot imagine any heavenly firm of brokers that might consent to arrange me a meeting with her beyond the grave," and that the Fialta meeting is the last one. He soon creates for us an image of Nina that intimates her impending death: "Had I to submit before judges of our earthly existence a specimen of her average pose, I would have perhaps placed her leaning upon a counter at Cook's, left calf crossing right shin, left toe tapping floor, sharp elbows and coin-spilling bag on the counter, while the employee, pencil in hand, pondered with her over the plan of an eternal sleeping car" (127).

This passage, which combines the very ordinariness of that Cook's counter, the vivid but unremarkable tapping of Nina's toe, the spilling handbag, the helpful clerk, and suddenly and poignantly juxtaposes all of them with that "eternal sleeping car," is a characteristic example of Nabokov's handling of a potentially troublesome artistic effect. The deft irony with which the commonplace scene at a Cook's counter breeds from its own ordinary elements—the sleeping car itself being of course the most clever and significant—a fresh image of death and loss, is representative of Nabokov's habitual strategy. He is always dealing with the most romantic and melodramatic of themes, and only the equilibrium of his wit, the irreverent comic touches, the purposely humdrum details can control our reactions to what might have been sentimental, obvious, or enfeebled by overuse. Just as with his use of parody, here Nabokov's use of irony, his refusal to insist on a single and solemn meaning, and his oblique, witty, surprising angle of presentation allow him to retain an effect without an appeal to us to disengage our intelligence, sense of realism, or prior artistic experience.

Nabokov has chosen to have Nina's automobile crash into a circus wagon, and this choice is, again, a matter of establishing cohesion within his story: a circus involves the movement of heavy vehicles and, more important, advertises itself in advance. Nabokov plants six different images of its approach to Fialta that fatal day, and the final stroke of the story—the revelation for Victor that Nina has been killed in the accident—unites and justifies these images, creates out of them the design which fate, or the artist who creates fate, had been completing all along just beyond the reach of Victor's perceptions. By giving us a foreknowledge of Nina's death, Nabokov softens our reaction to her; for against the vacuum of death, her vitality is poignant, and the "lies, the futility, the gibberish" that were part of her seem insignificant. The realization that Nina is to die makes any scrupulous judgment on her life irrelevant and almost ugly; one of the advantages that Nabokov derives from our foreknowledge is this numbing of our moral judgment, and it is an advantage he also exploits in *Lolita*. Nina's quiddities and the narrator's observations have the importance we accord to doomed things—an importance which comes from our realization that any random Something is preferable to that one sure Nothing, the eternal sleeping car.

Nabokov's most comprehensive self-criticism appears in a conversation Fyodor imagines himself having with the mysterious Koncheyev, his rival poet in *The Gift*. Koncheyev enumerates Fyodor-Nabokov's faults as Nabokov himself sees them:

"First, an excessive trust in words. It sometimes happens that your words in order to introduce the necessary thought have to smuggle it in. . . . Secondly . . . [you seem] undecided whether to enforce your style on past speeches and events or to make their own more salient. . . . Thirdly, you sometimes bring up parody to such a degree of naturalness that it actually becomes a genuine serious thought, but on *this* level it suddenly falters. . . . Fourthly, one observes in . . . your transitions something mechanical . . . which suggests you are pursuing *your own* advantage. . . . Fifthly and finally, you sometimes say things chiefly calculated to prick your contemporaries, but any woman can tell you that nothing gets lost so easily as a hairpin."[5]

It should not be surprising, then, that the individual elements in the story "Spring in Fialta" assume a vivaciousness in excess of their function. The circus poster in the following vignette is, on the narrative level, merely one more clue among several that a circus is coming to Fialta, but the addition of this clue to our semiconsciousness, a detail that will give an illusion of causality to the accident we discover in the story's last line, does not require the elaboration that Nabokov gives to it: "On our way to the hotel, we passed a half-built white villa, full of litter within, on a wall of which again the same elephants, their monstrous baby knees wide apart, sat on huge, gaudy drums; in ethereal bundles the equestrienne (already with a pencilled mustache) was resting on a broad-backed steed; and a tomato-nosed clown was walking a tightrope, balancing an umbrella ornamented with those recurrent stars—a vague symbolic recollection of the heavenly fatherland of circus performers" (138).

The elaboration of the image, and it is the fifth such circus image up to this point in the story, cannot be explained by the requirements of its function as a unit in this series of clues that will be revealed at last as Fate's design for Nina. Nabokov clearly delights in the image for its own sake. A real distortion starts to appear if we try to justify and reorganize and realign those aspects of his work that are not of the same size, depth, or verisimilitude as the narrative from which they are imperfectly suspended. Nabokov is aware of the powerful centripetal forces in his own art, and he has no use for prolonged invisibility. Just as with the academics in *Bend Sinister*, Nabokov will opportunistically seize a supernumerary to ventriloquize through him a phrase or image for which he can find no ready excuse within the dominant narrative voice. Here in "Spring in Fialta," something lovely demands to be said about Nina, and so the narrator overhears on a terrace one man saying to another: " 'Funny, how they all smell alike, burnt leaf through whatever perfume they use, those angular dark-haired girls,' and as it often happens, a trivial remark related to some unknown topic coiled and clung to one's own intimate recollection, a parasite of its sadness" (142).

This eavesdropping is not even vaguely believable; it is obviously created for its own sake and "disguised" with Olympian disdain. In Nabokov's fiction, we should always be aware of this indifference to mimicry and disguise and objectivity and organic relationships and consistent tone and singular verisimilar plane. In "Spring in Fialta," the exigencies of the plot do not prevent

Victor from delivering a distinctly Nabokovian aside of only
tenuous relevance to the themes and motion of the story itself:

After a brief period of fashionable religious conversion, during which
grace descended upon [Ferdinand] and he undertook some rather
ambiguous pilgrimages, which ended in a decidedly scandalous ad-
venture, he had turned his dull eyes toward barbarous Moscow.
Now, frankly speaking, I have always been irritated by the complacent conviction that a ripple of stream of consciousness, a few
healthy obscenities, and a dash of communism in any old slop pail
will alchemically and automatically produce ultramodern literature;
and I will contend until I am shot that art as soon as it is brought
into contact with politics inevitably sinks to the level of any ideo-
logical trash. [139–140]

Using his own enumeration of flaws as a guide, Nabokov is
definitely "pursuing his own advantage," the statement is obviously "calculated to prick" his contemporaries, and he has "enforced" his style and predilections on an innocent character. To
Nabokov, there are effects that are more important than the
simple illusion of credibility a fictional character must generate.

Recurrence is used in this story not only for infiltrating our
consciousness with the approach of the circus in order to produce
an illusion of causality and for evolving the theme of art's antithesis to life and the arbitrary designs of fate (as emblemized by
the sinister Englishman); it is also used for refining the theme of
loss that is the emotional fulcrum of the story.

Then [Ferdinand's] attention was drawn by an unfortunate object
exhibited in a souvenir shop: a dreadful marble imitation of Mount
St. George showing a black tunnel at its base, which turned out to
be the mouth of an inkwell, and with a compartment for pens in the
semblance of railroad tracks. Open-mouthed, quivering, all agog
with sardonic triumph, he turned that dusty, cumbersome, and perfectly irresponsible thing in his hands, paid without bargaining, and

with his mouth still open came out carrying the monster. Like some autocrat who surrounds himself with hunchbacks and dwarfs, he would become attached to this or that hideous object; this infatuation might last from five minutes to several days or even longer if the thing happened to be animate. [135]

And after a lunch where Nina, "for the last time in her life, was busy eating the shellfish of which she was so fond," Victor discovers that the inkstand has already been discarded by Ferdinand and hopes it will be "adopted" by the waiter. This detail sketches in the trajectory Nina herself will take. Nina "happens to be animate," but Ferdinand cannot begin to understand that "modest but true" core within her, nor can she herself bring it to light, and her death is doubtless to him a matter almost of discard. Without making a simplistic equation yoking Nina with the inkstand, our consciousness is alerted by this detail to the emotional appeals the story sets out, both for and against: Ferdinand's indifference to the inkstand subtly invites our censure, or at least our suspicion, whereas Nina's futile effort to adapt herself to inkstandhood invites our pity. Again, because he is dealing with a story of almost fairytale simplicity, Nabokov achieves his best effects by indirection, allowing us to focus on the inkstand, the circus posters, or the Englishman in order to generate a premonition of loss and death, and avoiding a direct appeal to our sense of the pathetic—an appeal that runs a high risk of being sentimental.

A last aspect of "Spring in Fialta" that deserves mention because of its importance in the later work of Nabokov is the complex of feelings that he associates with sexuality and with respectability.

One of the sources of tension in the story is a feeling on Victor's part that he is drawn both to a respectable world—safe, wholesome, and recognizable—and to one represented by Nina, embodied in Nina, a world of "lies, futility, and gibberish," a world of fascinating sexuality, a world that spawns a Mariette, a Liza Wind, a Lolita, an Ada, and is entirely antithetical to, say, the world of Krug's wife or Joan Clements in *Pnin* or of Sybil Shade in *Pale Fire.* "Even in the absence of any sentimental discord, I felt myself bound to seek for a rational, if not moral, interpretation of my existence, and this meant choosing between the world in which I sat for my portrait, with my wife, my young daughters, the Dobermann pinscher (idyllic garlands, a signet ring, a slender cane), between that happy, wise, and good world . . . and what?" (137–138).

That "what" is of course precisely that which Humbert Humbert plunges into when he chooses Lilith over Eve, and it carries his sensitive moral consciousness back into a world of hideously delicious and forbidden sexuality. *Lolita* is the perfect expression of the beauty and horror of the theme, and the resolution of that novel is, as we shall see, the only triumph over it in all of Nabokov's fiction.

Julian Moynahan illuminates a major theme of Nabokov's moral world in a comment on marriage itself in his fiction:

Nabokov's great theme, which he shares with the Beethoven of *Fidelio* . . . is that of married love. In *Fidelio,* when Leonora penetrates to the dark dungeon where Florestan languishes in fetters and brings him up to light and freedom, she is acting out, in all the tenderness and courage of uxorious passion, a great moral positive that I find, either fulfilled or blighted, in all of Nabokov's major work. The connection is between loving and making free in a bond of two against the loneliness of exile, the imprisoning world, the irredeemable nature of time, the voidness of eternity. I am thinking of *The Gift,* that great wedding song, of widower Krug's agony of loss in *Bend Sinister,* of the sinister parodies of wedded states in *Kamera Obskura, Lolita,* and *King, Queen, Knave* . . . of the poor prisoner [Cincinnatus] in *Invitation*—that mock-*Fidelio*—cursed with a foolish unfaithful wife, of old John and Sybil Shade in *Pale Fire,* whose life together is such an irritating unfathomable mystery to the mad solitary neighbor spying on them from the shrubbery.[6]

The impulse toward uxoriousness is powerful in Nabokov's protagonists, but Victor's announcement of its pleasurable pressure and yet its distance, its secondariness, is also characteristic: "I had left my wife and children at home, and that was an island of happiness always present in the clear north of my being, always flotating beside me, and even through me, I dare say, but yet keeping on the outside of me most of the time" (122).

What Moynahan's comment seems to ignore is that the passionate, illicit, contrary impulse is also often embodied in Nabokov's protagonists—Victor "sits for his portrait" with burgherish dutifulness, but his heart belongs to la belle dame sans merci, Nina. This impulse constantly strains against the "happy and wise" world of daughters and sunshine and Dobermans, and at last finds its most comprehensive expression in a prolonged, horrific copulation with that eerie child-woman in the Komfy Kabins of the American republic. In "Spring in Fialta," reading backward from *Lolita,* written a decade and a half later, we find intimations that Nabokov has created, by a kind of fission, his Victor and his Ferdinand, two types that we find at first fused in Humbert Humbert, but which later separate into a Humbert Humbert who is redeemable and a Clare Quilty who is not. Ferdinand, the sinister esthete who enthralls and helps to destroy Nina, seems related to Humbert. One of the minor scenes in "Spring in Fialta" is inescapably prototypical of the theme of *Lolita:* "Further on, near a fountain, Ferdinand gave his stick of candy to a native child, a swarthy girl with beads around her pretty neck; we stopped to wait for him: he crouched, saying something to her, addressing her sooty-black lowered eyelashes, and then he caught up with us, grinning and making one of those remarks with which he loved to spice his speech" (134–135).

The "sooty-black" lashes of the native child will later belong to Dolores Haze, and the adult with his bribe of candy and the girl behind those downcast lashes will become the whole tragedy itself.

"Triangle within Circle"

The alliance between the inner core of fairytale and the surface attributes of realism is a constant in Nabokov's art; without the irony which the realism contributes to the fairytale, that is, the control of tone which is one of the most useful contributions of irony, the fairytale would probably be unacceptable. A former student of Nabokov's, Ross Wetzsteon, remembers Nabokov's making the claim that "great novels are above all great fairy tales."[7] The "fantastically deceitful and complex" qualities that Nabokov attributes to art, especially his own art, are attributes which describe the complex interrelationship of the parts, images, details, or planes of illusion and "reality" within his work much more successfully than they can describe the moral oppositions in it— for the moral oppositions are absolutely distinct, the appeals unambiguous, and we rarely have any difficulty in discovering where our sympathies should lie. Good opposes Evil, the Sensitive clashes with the Brutal, Folly breeds its own fatality. Simplicity and inevitability are givens. We are made to sense, just below the surface, that thrilling and frightening world, peculiar to the fairytale, of things at last behaving as we have always wished or feared they would behave rather than behaving as they do, the ascendency of the emotional fact—magic—over the empirical.

But Nabokov's task is more fundamental than simply disguising a fairytale; he must show how the fairytale works itself out amid the attributes and possibilities of the unsimple world of the non-fairytale—our world, our consciousness, which contains but exceeds the fairytale. Of course, we are always trying to make fairytales live in this world. I would venture to say that Nabokov would find Buchenwald a kind of fairytale, not only because he derives from it Paduk's monstrous state (which is one pole of the *Bend Sinister* fairytale), but because the Final Solution is, in a sense, a naive attempt to work out in the real world, which is never final and has no solutions, a fairytale idea of good and evil: if all the Jews are destroyed, a positive sort of good will be accomplished—and accomplished once and for all. The horror of the extermination camp is thus the incompatibility of fantasy and context, fairytale and world.

The sinister bends that Nabokov sees life taking are a matter of this grotesque incompatibility of things in terms of their appropriateness and possibilities and intensity: Linda and Mariette Bachofen talking over, with "limp schoolgirl gestures," Linda's lover being beaten to death in the bathroom; Krug and Cincinnatus at last simply walking off the preposterous stage set which they had thought to be their world; Paduk reducing his appearance and his thought to a hard-edged Oldenberg cartoon of an Everyman; John Shade dying from a madman's bullet to which he is irrelevant—these represent the way in which Nabokov perceives this incompatibility and its consequences. It is futile to talk of Nabokov's characters as if their moral choices and experiences affected their fate, or as if they moved in a rational milieu. Character and world, illusion and reality are incompatible and, like grafts or transplants, they reject each other, with fatal results. "Triangle Within Circle" pivots on this incompatibility and its consequences.

In *Speak, Memory,* recounting a last visit in Switzerland to his aging childhood governess, an old and deaf Frenchwoman he calls Mademoiselle O., Nabokov describes a vision about her life and her death that signifies to him something quite profound and yet not quite paraphrasable. On visiting Mademoiselle with a hearing aid he has bought with money loaned to him by a friend, Nabokov discovers that it does not help the old woman's deafness and that she has lied to him about it in order to please him. This anecdote verges on sentimentality, and sentimentality represents a failure of perception, but the vision of the swan that Nabokov juxtaposes to it generates real pathos, and evokes for us a Mademoiselle that we perceive and pity without false coloration or manipulated emotions—a much more powerful and important experience:

Before leaving for Basle and Berlin, I happened to be walking along the lake in the cold, misty night. At one spot a lone light dimly diluted the darkness and transformed the mist into a visible drizzle. *"Il pleut toujours en Suisse"* was one of those casual comments which, formerly, had made Mademoiselle weep. Below, a wide ripple, almost a wave, and something vaguely white attracted my eye. As I came quite close to the lapping water, I saw that it was—an aged swan, a large, uncouth, dodo-like creature, making ridiculous efforts to hoist himself into a moored boat. He could not do it. . . . Although I soon forgot that dismal night . . . that compound image—shudder and swan and swell . . . first came to my mind when a couple of years later I learned that Mademoiselle had died . . .

Have I really salvaged her from fiction? Just before the rhythm I hear falters and fades, I catch myself wondering whether, during the years I knew her, I had not kept utterly missing something in her that was far more she than her chins or her ways or even her French—something perhaps akin to that last glimpse of her, to the radiant deceit she had used in order to have me depart pleased with my own kindness, or to that swan whose agony was so much closer to artistic truth than a drooping dancer's pale arms.[8]

This vision combines a creature from the world of the fairy-tale—a swan—with elements that are both painfully realistic and comic. This combining of realistic surface detail with subsurface fairytale elements is typical of Nabokov's artistic practice. The swan grades into a "drooping dancer" on the sentimental side of the artistic spectrum and into a "dodo" on the ludicrous side, and Nabokov insists on both, on all of the experience. The agonies of other aging swans—Krug, Humbert, Pnin, John Shade, Van Veen—will at last become the central concern of Nabokov's fiction, and countervailing the potential dangers of sentimentality, Nabokov will insist on presenting them webs and all.

"Triangle within Circle"[9] is the story of young and very ludicrous swans: three university people, two men and a girl, who form a suicide pact. The three are bound by both friendship—the circle—and, within that circle of friendship and "eroding its circumference," the triangle of unrequited agony, a combination of their heterosexual and homosexual love that perfectly cancels sexual contact: Yasha loves Rudolf, Rudolf loves the Russian girl Olya, and Olya, of course, loves Yasha. They decide to kill themselves, but only Yasha actually does so, and his suicide has a remarkable effect on his parents. The plot consists only of this, but the story is much more powerful than the simple and primitive skeleton would lead us to expect.

The connection between the story and the novel in which it appears, *The Gift,* is relatively tenuous. Fyodor Godunov-Cherdynstev, the protagonist of the novel, relates the tale to us as merely the banal and unpromising raw material for a story or novel. The story quickly asserts its own life, however, and the connections Fyodor has with it as narrator are summarily dismissed for a more omniscient voice—one nearer to Nabokov's own. We will even have that shameless device of the hard-pressed storyteller, direct quotations from a diary.

The diary is Yasha's, and Yasha is the authorial favorite; and, as Fyodor's voice tells us, it is sensitive Yasha who defines the circle and the fatal triangle within the circle. But Fyodor finds the story a "banal triangle of tragedy," and goes on to say that "the mere presence of such suspiciously neat structure, to say nothing of the fashionable counterpoint of its development, would never have permitted me to make it into a short story or a novel" (54–55).

Since Fyodor-Nabokov proceeds to tell the story anyway, Fyodor's statement may first impress us as a clumsy trick on Nabokov's part, merely another instance of "smuggling." But Nabokov does not attempt to make this story into an organic component of the larger novel in which it appears—obviously the intrinsic possibilities of the story are what fascinate him and should fascinate us. Fyodor's huffy comment provides a distance between the telling and any unqualified approval of the tale, and this distance is essential to Nabokov's tone.

We have seen Nabokov use tone as a protective device before. Equating Mademoiselle with an agonized swan could be banal, sentimental, overlovely, unreal—it could be bad art. Instead, Mademoiselle's life and death are made real and moving because the swan is a real swan, as much a "dodo" as a dancer, or more of one, and the agonies of age and impotence and desire are expressed in an image of what we know them to be, rather than as the falsifications of sentimentality would present them. So, too, in the short story, Nabokov makes sure that our judgment is no more stringent than his own, and he uses various intonations, intrusions, and details to ensure a full spectrum of meaning. " 'I am fiercely in love with the soul of Rudolf,' wrote Yasha in his agitated, neoromantic style. 'I love its harmonious proportions, its health, the joy it has in living. I am fiercely in love with this naked, suntanned, lithe soul, which has an answer to everything and proceeds through life as a self-confident woman does across a ballroom floor. . . . [But] this is just as fruitless as falling in love with the moon' " (55).

Nabokov displaces Yasha's desires slightly away from mere physical homosexuality toward a yearning more spiritual: Yasha admiringly claims that Rudolf's soul "has an answer to everything." I think we are to feel that the surety in Rudolph toward which Yasha experiences an adolescent attraction is the kind that Ekwilism or Catholicism or Nazism or Communism provides to the masses. These philosophies are able to tell us what to do with the troublesome problems of consciousness, conscience, desire, impurity, or life itself; all problems have been anticipated, all solutions outlined. In life, or in Nabokov, dogma is endlessly seductive and, at least in the latter, always destructive. Yasha's yearning is merely a variant on the essential directionless spiritual energy supposed universally common to youth, but the consequences of his passions, which are youthful and foolish, and his honesty and resolve, which are mature and admirable, lead him to pursue his illusion right into his own death. Even Nina thinks she has at least a slim chance, but Yasha is unsparing of himself and knows, on one level at least, exactly where his passionate truthfulness will lead. He is foolish and heroic. Both his foolishness and his heroism are essential to Nabokov's effect.

Nabokov, plumping almost overtly for his favorite, tells us that "if one looks at the matter more closely, one suspects that Yasha's passion was perhaps not so abnormal after all" (55), and he goes on to compare it with the adolescent hero-worship a generation of Russian boys felt toward the entire generation and class of idealistic "future martyrs"—the intelligentsia who both brought on, and were exterminated by, the Revolution.

But Rudolf is not "a teacher, a martyr, or a leader," and the "answer" he seems to possess is really only the smugness of one who never poses a question. He is the most sinister type Nabokov can conjure up, "a so-called 'Bursch,' a German 'regular guy,' notwithstanding a certain propensity for obscure poetry, lame music, lopsided art—which did not affect him in that fundamental soundness by which Yasha was captivated, or thought he was" (55). Nabokov has drawn his essential distinction between the "sound" man of groups, Rudolf, a German, and the isolated, unstable man, Yasha, a displaced Russian. The nationalities are important, of course, an invariable Nabokovian code, and we are unconfused as to which one will claim our sympathy—and which one will be destroyed. Rudolf falls in love with Olya "on the lowest level, primitively and impatiently" (56). Again, the physicality, what Humbert Humbert does not deign to describe because it is "mere animality," forms one of Nabokov's primary poles of feeling and judgment. Yasha, at least, is in love with an idea, an answer—a false answer, but a real enough desire. For Rudolf, Nabokov has no sympathy at all.

Meanwhile Olya, unchivalrously described as "an indolent, grasping, and morosely freakish girl," has fallen in love with Yasha. This is the story's given, and the givens of fairytales are nothing if not trite, but Nabokov's agent Fyodor, in expressing for us that oppressive and limiting triteness, deliberately cancels it. He describes Yasha, Rudolf, and Olya in terms of the "*dramatis personae* of eighteenth-century French playwrights" (56) and labels the three of them "X," "Y," and "Z."

Thus an academic and formal distance is established between the teller and his tale. Fyodor-Nabokov is careful not to take all the responsibility for the banality of his creations—not only to evade a charge of banality, but to maintain judgment and perspective, and to ensure that we share them, too.

The young people soon develop a code alluding to their common problem and then, "with all the rapture of frankness, . . . jointly discuss their feelings with all three present" (56–57). Although their parents suspect nothing, "something doomful" is growing among the three, a phenomenon that Nabokov does not present center-stage, for he suddenly reveals to us, in the oblique manner that he exercises when he senses thin ice, that there are no angels "already converging, already swarming and fussing professionally around the cradle"—the cradle in which there lies "a dark little newborn revolver" (57). Fyodor-Nabokov's distance from, and disapproval of, the burden of this tale, a tale he won't even tell since it's too trite, obviate the necessity of explaining why all three simultaneously decide that suicide is their only solution. The little revolver is a fact, and that is all we are going to be told. It is no more complicated than a magic pumpkin or Rapunzel's hair.

The general idea—hence, the master illusion—of the suicide pact is to cancel out the sexual relationships among the three that, if physically requited, would bring jealous sorrow to all of them, and also to enable them to go to a place wherein "an ideal and flawless circle might be restored"; the overvoice tells us in mock-ignorance that, although it is "hard to determine who first proposed it and when," this idea of leaving a realm of sexual desire and torment for another, better one of spirit is "developed most actively" by Olya, and that Yasha takes on a role befitting his own personality and dilemma, that of poet laureate of the triangle. We should be well warned of what happens to the sensitive favorite in most of Nabokov's work.

All three have signed over their wills to fate, and that fate begins to pick up speed in order to reach its destination on time. Typically trite, Olya picks the eighteenth anniversary of her father's death—even their mysticism and their fatidic date are banal—and the three set out for Berlin's Grunewald, carrying, of course, the revolver, "which had become by now quite burly and independent."

Because this is the ride to the gallows, Nabokov runs the tramcar past us at less than twenty-four frames per second, and it is no accident that at this point, after everything has been settled once and for all, the description of physical details is the most elaborate: "Yasha's big-peaked cap, which he had not worn for about four years and had for some reason put on today, gave him an oddly plebeian look; Rudolf was hatless and the wind ruffled his blond hair, thrown back from his temples; Olya stood leaning against the rear railing, gripping the black stang with a white, firm hand that had a prominent ring on its index finger—and gazed with narrowed eyes at the streets flicking by, and all the time kept stepping by mistake on the treadle of the gentle little bell in the floor (intended for the huge, stonelike foot of the motorman when the rear of the car became the front)" (58).

In spite of the narrator's announced intentions never to tell the story, it is told. But the narrator's voice has become that of an omniscient, creative deity. The wind that "ruffled [Rudolf's] blond hair"; Olya stepping on the little bell; that "oddly plebeian" look of Yasha in his old cap—these are details logically unavailable to Fyodor, who was not physically at the scene.

The pretense of indifference and disapproval with which the initial stages of the story are related is a defensive measure—defending the intelligence and potency of the overvoice, Fyodor-Nabokov, from a charge of banality. But once past the possibilities of silliness, triteness, predictability, and overperfection that are the inescapable dangers of melodrama and fairytale, the voice finds itself free to discover the "modest but true core" that resides in the particular detail, image, feeling, and expression. The obligation to maintain the narrative point of view available to

Fyodor, who would have been prevented by the laws of time and physics from observing what he so precisely describes, is indifferently cast aside in favor of the possibilities open only to the omniscient overvoice. Nabokov is an opportunist in his art.

On the streetcar the three meet a cousin of Yasha's, Yuily Posner, "an alert, self-confident person," who gives Yasha his new address on his card and reminds Yasha to remind a cousin to return some books. The effect of this little episode is astonishing: "A certain mysterious change had occurred: by the act of leaving them alone, although only for a minute (Posner and his daughter got off very soon), Yasha had, as it were, broken the alliance and had initiated his separation from them, so that when he rejoined them on the platform he was, though as much unaware of it as they were, already on his own and the invisible crack, in keeping with the law governing all cracks, continued irresistibly to creep and widen" (59).

Once out in the enormous Grunewald park, they "got down to business; to be more exact, Yasha got down to business: he had that honesty of spirit that imparts to the most reckless act an almost everyday simplicity." Again, the overvoice is plumping for its favorite—the kiss of death. "He said he would shoot himself first by right of seniority (he was a year older than Rudolf and a month older than Olya) and this simple remark rendered unnecessary the stroke of drawn lots, which, in its coarse blindness, would probably have fallen on him anyway . . ." (59).

Notice the speculation that the lots would probably have selected him to go first; behind the surface of things there is always a meddlesome and contriving mystery that singles out its proper victim—the tender and sensitive.

The shot is a "dull pop," Yasha's life is over, and "here dusk begins to fall on the story. . . . Rudolf, whether because a certain terrestrial vacancy had opened for him or because he was simply a coward, lost all desire to shoot himself" (60). Olya is powerless to kill herself because Rudolf hides the revolver. The overvoice is by implication again at the mercy of a dreadfully trite tale: "Rumor has it that it was then that they became lovers, but this would be really too flat" (61).

The mother of Yasha is transformed by his suicide. Her grief takes on an "industrious, even enraptured" passion, she becomes almost professional in her mourning. Even Olya's failure to share this exalted state of grief with her (Olya is "morosely polite, morosely impatient" when Yasha's mother comes to see her) does not interfere with the eerie enjoyment that now displaces all other concerns for the bereaved old woman.

Her husband's reaction is much less happy, and even more eerie: "Yasha's death had its most painful effect on his father. He had to spend the whole summer in a sanatorium and he never really recovered: the partition dividing the room temperature of reason from the infinitely ugly, cold, ghostly world into which Yasha has passed suddenly crumbled, and to restore it was impossible, so that the gap had to be draped in makeshift fashion and one tried not to look at the stirring folds" (61).

The stories "Lance" and "Signs and Symbols" deal with mad sons and grieving parents, and John Shade must deal with the suicide of his daughter in *Pale Fire*. Fyodor's father has vanished somewhere in Central Asia in *The Gift*, and the narrator of *The Real Life of Sebastian Knight* is recreating the life of a dead half-brother. Krug's wife and son are both destroyed. Pnin has his Mira Belochkin, Humbert his Annabel by the sea, who perishes "of typhus in Corfu." Aqua Veen, hopelessly mad, commits suicide in *Ada*. Clearly Nabokov is interested in inflicting a maximum of suffering on his creations: there can be no value without loss, and Nabokov is always involved with the most profound questions of value.

3

Pale Fire

"A witch's sabbath of European words within a ruined mind within a meager, complacent community;"[1] "a combination between an operetta by Franz Lehar and some early Marx Brothers film"[2]—these are both unarguable, if inconclusive, descriptions of *Pale Fire*.

The structural oddity of this story of an aging dodo-swan is nicely defined by Nina Berberova: "There is in *Pale Fire* a structural surprise: the symbolic level, the fantastic, the poetic, lies on the surface and is obvious, while the factual, the realistic is only slightly hinted at, and may be approached as a riddle. The realistic level is hidden by the symbolic one which has nothing enigmatic in it and is immediately clear to the reader."[3]

On one level the story concerns the death of poet John Shade. Short one line of completing his autobiographical poem "Pale Fire," Shade is mistaken for his neighbor, an infamous judge, and is shot to death by a lunatic murderer, Jack Grey, who has come to revenge himself on that judge.

John Shade's companion, Charles Kinbote, a bizzarre émigré homosexual who has attached himself to Shade and Shade's university, confiscates the poem and issues it with a Commentary and an Index appended to its 999 lines and 499-and-½ couplets. The unholy relationship of Kinbote's Commentary to Shade's poem is the point of departure for this witch's sabbath of words and Marx Brothers operetta.

John Shade, like Krug, is the darling of the author, and he displays not only the characteristics we always recognize in Nabokov's favorites—genius, compassion, reverence for detail, love of Shakespeare, vulnerability, curiosity, extremely tender paternal instincts—but the limitations of the type as well. Like Krug, he can think and create, but his actions are severely circumscribed since he is beyond career ambitions, is happily uxorious, and is indifferent to any social organism.

Like Krug, he will lose his child, and this loss is central to the poem he writes. Again like Krug, he will die prematurely—a fate Nabokov inflicts on nearly all his favorites.

The most interesting achievements and most revealing failures of *Pale Fire* are connected with the uses of voice; but the relation of the parts, the characters, and the levels of reality in the novel is so complex that it might be best to look first at Shade and later at the assassin Gradus as descendants of Krug and Paduk, respectively, and as the poles of the novel's human types.

In *Pale Fire,* a dramatic impasse is created by Nabokov's choice of an overperfect protagonist, the authorial equivalent John Shade, who has no important failings or problems except those of the artist; and the problems of the artist are, by definition, nondramatic. We get nothing less than a major creation of Shade's, the poem "Pale Fire," and the intellectual and emotional burdens of this poem have a good deal of substance and interest in themselves.

In order to give his equivalent individuality, Nabokov endows him with a "wobbly heart . . . a slight limp, and a certain curious contortion in his method of progress"; the old poet reads, to narrator Kinbote's horror, "a tabloid newspaper which I had thought no poet would deign to touch" (22). When Shade's colleague Hurley twitted him about a "stunning blonde in black leotards" in his class, Shade, healthily heterosexual, "all his wrinkles beaming, benignly tapped Hurley on the wrist to make him stop" (21). Shade is nothing if not lovable.

As a spiritually flawless Nabokovian equivalent, Shade is used to paraphrase Nabokov's own pronouncements on various subjects. For example, in his *Playboy* interview, Nabokov said that he "automatically gave low marks when a student used the dreadful phrase 'sincere and simple'—under the impression that this was the greatest compliment payable to prose or poetry."[4] As a parallel, we find Shade saying to Kinbote: "I am also in the habit of lowering a student's mark catastrophically if he uses 'simple' and 'sincere' in a commendatory sense" (156). This sort of paraphrase occurs several times, and although the pronouncements are of course intelligent, fresh, and nonsimple (as well as sincere), Nabokov's predilection, for moral, intellectual, and spiritual flawlessness in his protagonists badly weakens his resources for dramatic involvement. The danger for his novels is that the sense of ethical and moral preposterousness the author and his equivalents hold for the absurd villains that surround them threatens to trivialize the evil forces. This trivialization occurs in *Invitation to a Beheading,* where it is part of the intention, and in *Pale Fire,* where it is also part of the intention but perhaps should not have been. In *Bend Sinister,* our historical awareness of what totalitarian dictatorships do with maverick intellectuals is alerted, and this contributes dramatic tension to Krug's prolonged refusal to take Paduk seriously merely because the dictator is absurd.

Speaking of a Cambridge friend's enthusiasm for Lenin in the 1920's, Nabokov summarizes a great deal of his own inky political philosophy with the laconic statement that "[my friend] never realized that had he and other foreign idealists been

Russians in Russia, he and they would have been destroyed by
Lenin's regime as naturally as rabbits are by ferrets and
farmers,"[5] and the Darwinian force behind the adverb "naturally"
expresses a good deal of Nabokov's contempt for the optimistic
naiveté of Western intellectuals. Krug's resistance to the total
state that wants his mind seems to him the act of a rational and
free intelligence against absurd and disgusting monstrosities; but
we as readers in a historical context know very well indeed that
those "jack-booted baboons" are powerful in direct proportion to
their indifference to truth, freedom, and human life. Nabokov
makes us believe in Paduk's state; it is claustrophobic, vicious,
and real. More real to us than to Krug, who is ignorant of
Buchenwald.

Come to arrest Ember, Hustav tells Krug: "There is really
nothing special about this weapon. A humdrum official article,
No. 184682, of which you can see dozens any time." And Krug
replies, with a depth of sincerity: "I think I have had enough of
this. . . . I do not believe in pistols."(111).

Krug's nonbelief concerning the purposes for which "humdrum
No. 184682" has been designed amounts to moral incredulity
concerning murder, political and physical. We recall Kinbote
admitting, for Nabokov, a dead-end to his inquiry into the mind
of Gradus: "Our Lord has fashioned man so marvellously that no
amount of motive hunting and rational inquiry can ever *really*
explain how and why anybody is capable of destroying a fellow
creature" (279). In both novels, the protagonists cannot understand the fact of murder. The moral plane on which Krug and
Shade exist is different from that of the Paduks and Graduses,
who commit murder without hesitation or regret.

In the key passage in which Nabokov explains Pnin's refusal to
allow any reality to Mira's death at Buchenwald, the overvoice
claims that "no *conscience*, and hence no *consciousness*" (italics

mine) could deal with that outrageous fact. The extermination camp, Paduk, Gradus, the secret police and their humdrum little No. 184682's, torture, assassination, murder itself are not morally apprehensible in Nabokov's created worlds, and this is one of the most important differences between those worlds and the worlds of *1984* or *Darkness at Noon,* where the police apparatus still involves human desire and personality, still involves the self and a sense of will, and where evil, cruelty, and corruption are still located on the same human continuum as goodness, compassion, or purity. In *1984* or *Darkness at Noon,* the experience of each protagonist is one of conversion; in Nabokov's totalitarian worlds, the authorial equivalent and his group, and the murderous agents and their group are separated by an unbridgeable gulf and no conversion is possible; in Nabokov, the dark forces are not really any more analyzable than are a wolf or a witch from the Brothers Grimm. Further, the alliance between consciousness and conscience in the passage from *Pnin* is extremely significant: in Nabokov's worlds, to have consciousness is to be *morally* conscious.

Thus when Nabokov accepts only an art-for-art's-sake definition of his work, no indifference to human values should be inferred. He is simply refusing any exterior system of value, utility, theme, or message and is defensively insisting that his work is about nothing except itself. The tale he tells us, again and again, is the tale of the sensitive consciousness and its clash with the inadmissible brute fact—the "prison bars of time," the bestial dictator, the kerosene-soaked saplings on which tender and beautiful human beings are burned like carrion, the wave of grief and pain, unbearable because it has no logical meaning, that annihilates the consciousness required to deal with it. "Now we take all this, press it into a small ball, and fit it into the centre of Krug's brain where it gently expands" (197), the overvoice of

Bend Sinister relates to us, after Krug has learned David has been turned over to the inmates. And the expansion, if gentle, is inexorable, and very, very thorough.

Objective and Subjective

A minor difficulty in speaking about Gradus as an assassin is that, on one plane within *Pale Fire,* he does not exist; he is, we learn through various clues in the novel, a fantasy, private to Kinbote; Shade's destroyer is the vengeful lunatic Jack Grey, who fatally mistakes Shade for Judge Goldsworth. This discovery about the "Gradus" whom Kinbote has projected into synchronization with the creation of the poem "Pale Fire," and whose ominous approach we have been watching throughout the novel, would seem to be enough to reduce the entire Gradus design to an insignificant fantasy. But our reaction to the discovery does not trivialize the impact. Gradus as assassin is as "real" in the novel as Krug is real in his story, and Nabokov fully intends that the life and the poetry and the rationality and the value of John Shade are to be juxtaposed with the forces of antilife and absurdity and antivalue embodied in the grubby little gunman, who drips with diarrhea as he stumbles through the makeshift arrangements of fate to perform for Nabokov the esthetically desirable task of eliminating John Shade from the fiction to which he is dramatically irrelevant.

In other words, Gradus is real in moral and esthetic terms, if not in objective ones. His meaning and presence in the novel are not canceled for us merely because we discover he is not of the same plane of reality as Shade—just as Krug's tragedy is not dismissed because he is merely a character in a book. Fiction is never more nor less than fiction, and our response to it does not question its right to insist on its own artificiality.

But the fate that destroys Shade—whether an assassin from

Zembla bent on destroying Kinbote or a lunatic killer destroying Judge Goldsworth's look-alike—is simply not a convincing device, and Nabokov's use of it is gratuitous. The problem with Shade's destruction is that it is an arbitrary act for which we hold Nabokov, not Gradus, responsible. Shade is useful to Nabokov as a voice, but as an actor he is a liability. This distinction is crucial in reading *Pale Fire*.

Shade is deeply involved with death at a much more meaningful level than the administrative one that Gradus represents. His presence and function in the novel have no dramatic relevance but only emotional and philosophical significance. He wants nothing the world can provide. In other words, Shade's voice is necessary as a vehicle for certain kinds of emotion (mostly in respect to the death of his daughter), and his voice is necessary for the asking of the philosophical questions that interest Nabokov, but Shade is not fully engaged in the novel's activity, and his reality is not quite subsumed into its frame. This problem will become more apparent later on when we look at Nabokov's use of voice.

Both Krug and Shade, like many of Nabokov's other favorites, are endlessly cross-examining life and death in order to get some rudimentary answers. Krug fails; Nabokov even enforces the fictionality of his favorite character, his never-livingness, in the novel's last passage, and admits that the "immortality" he has conferred upon Krug is merely "a play upon words." But even within the confines of his own consciousness, Krug-as-character cannot come to terms with death. We are told that when both his parents were killed in an automobile accident, Krug had to fight for his sanity against this horror, and won a temporary reprieve. "With one strong shrug of his burly shoulders he shook off the burden of sanctity enveloping the monster [death], and as with a thump and a great explosion of dust the thick old mats and carpets and things fell, he had experienced a kind of hideous relief. But could he do it again?" (122).

He cannot win another reprieve, of course; he is reduced to insanity, then further reduced by his creator to a simple illusion. But Nabokov does not pretend that he can create life, that his creative powers parallel those of his Creator. Krug's philosophy is something called "creative destruction," as we have seen. "But he also knew that what people saw in him . . . was not an admirable expansion of positive matter but a kind of inaudible frozen explosion (as if the reel had been stopped at the point where the bomb bursts) with some debris gracefully poised in mid-air" (154).

Krug can get no further with the problems that vexed the ancients (and vex Nabokov) than the mournful display of "a cold little heap of truisms fished out of the artificial lake, which they had been especially put for the purpose" (154), and he can say only that death is "either the instantaneous gaining of perfect knowledge . . . or absolute nothingness, *nichto*" (155–156). This inconclusive formulation is such a dismal show Krug leaves off the questioning. Long before his final tragedy takes shape, he has been digging himself that pit of "pure smiling madness" which the possessors of intelligence and honesty and possibilities always dig for themselves in Nabokov's world.

Shade is also metaphysically vexed; his poem, indeed, his function as a separate voice within the novel exist to ask the question: Why this life? Why so much tenderness and such sensations if they are to be merely consigned to the humiliating *nichto* of the nonsense grave? Unlike Krug, Shade finds a kind of answer.

> I feel I understand
> Existence, or at least a minute part
> Of my existence, only through my art,
> In terms of combinational delight;

And if my private universe scans right,
So does the verse of galaxies divine
Which I suspect is an iambic line.
I'm reasonably sure that we survive
And that my darling somewhere is alive.

[Canto Four, 11.971–979]

But Shade still looks for more than just a "minute part of [his] existence." Having suffered a vision of a fountain during a heart attack, he reads a magazine article in which it is written that another heart attack victim saw a fountain, too. But it is a typographical error—he discovers the other victim hasn't seen a fountain, but a mountain. Everything he had hoped to believe is, for the moment, impossible. If both of them had seen a fountain, this would have confirmed that both of them had experienced something objective in the darkness that limits our mortality.

Our fountain was a signpost and a mark
Objectively enduring in the dark,
Strong as a bone, substantial as a tooth,
And almost vulgar in its robust truth!

[Canto Three, 11.763–766]

And now: "Life Everlasting—based on a misprint!" The misprint, however, leads Shade to an even more subtle speculation about the signs and symbols left by the organizing power. The misprint was only evidence that the game was more intricate than he had expected it to be—but there is *still* a game, with two sets of intelligences playing it: one of them our own human consciousness; the other, the antagonist, some undreamed-of force indescribable to logic and sensuous perception:

It did not matter who they were. No sound
No furtive light came from their involute
Abode, but there they were, aloof and mute,

Playing a game of worlds, promoting pawns
To ivory unicorns and ebon fauns;
Kindling a long life here, extinguishing
A short one there; killing a Balkan king;
Causing a chunk of ice formed on a high-
Flying airplane to plummet from the sky
And strike a farmer dead; hiding my keys,
Glasses or pipe. Coordinating these
Events and objects with remote events
And vanished objects. Making ornaments
Of accidents and possibilities.   [Canto Three 11.816–829]

This muted optimism is as far as Shade can honestly advance: he believes that there is a "game," that there is another sort of intelligence. He is unprepared to venture anything concerning the moral interests of that intelligence, to postulate a heaven or a hell.

The questions Shade asks and the conclusions he draws may well be those Nabokov himself approves, but the poem as poem suffers the same deficiency that afflicts most of Nabokov's verse: a forfeiture of his complex and multidimensional presentation to the demands of the form. As a rhyme scheme the couplet is particularly limiting for an artist whose prose is so much itself in its complications and its convolutions, its elegant rhetoric and sinuous articulation of sense, syntax, parenthesis, and thought. Nabokov is a sidewinder. His best prose is pictorial and usually very elaborate and witty; and he draws many of his memorable effects from vivacious imagery enriched by a comic underlighting of ironic, urbane qualification. Further, Nabokov is remarkably skillful in reproducing the effect of the mind itself at work, presenting the perceiving consciousness not only perceiving but mirroring itself as it does so. This strength is difficult to exercise in couplets.

The poem "Pale Fire" is a performance, an extended *tour de force*, rather than a first-rate piece of verse; Nabokov's mastery of the form itself seems to be part of his point, and it is this impulse toward bravura and his eagerness to accept the sheer challenge of the rhyme scheme that leave one uneasy about, and unconvinced by, the poem's narrative, emotional, and philosophical content. Here we have a case of the "unique rules" and "nightmare obstacles" which Nabokov's artist imposes upon himself in order to surmount them, rather than the free and thorough presentation of complex experience which Nabokov's best prose achieves.

When the Bureau of Pleasantrips or Paduk and his police form one pole of the conflict in Nabokov's fiction, we have a strong melodramatic conflict. *Bend Sinister, Invitation to a Beheading,* and "Cloud, Castle, Lake" represent this conflict most dramatically. But the weight and importance of Shade's involvement with the most painful and important questions about life and death on his own metaphysical terms make his clash with Gradus more a matter of stylization and metaphor than of blood, grief, and bullets. Shade has already been removed from the scene before he is killed by Gradus (or Jack Grey). He has completed his poem, and the poem itself resolves and summarizes the life of its creator in several ways, rendering Shade's physical death, even more than Krug's, a "matter of style."

The poem "Pale Fire" not only explicitly claims that a "game" is going on between us and some interested intelligence, but also that the creation of the poem itself represents the proper use of art, to tell "what has really happened in some way," as opposed to its improper use as ornament à la Ferdinand in "Spring in Fialta." Thus in "Pale Fire," Shade writes:

> I was the shadow of the waxwing slain
> By the false azure in the windowpane;
> I was the smudge of ashen fluff—and I
> Lived on, flew on, in the reflected sky. [Canto One, 11.1-4]

The poem itself is this "flying on"—flying on, in art, on the other side of the windowpane. And the windowpane is, again, the fatal membrane through which the merely physical cannot fly, and we have of course seen it before: the windowscreen that separates the world of time and death from the world of immortal art in *Bend Sinister's* last passage. As artist, Shade can create something immortal out of Hazel's physical death, and this represents the highest use of human consciousness, the use of art to make the universe "scan right."

Again and again in Nabokov's work we find reference to an intuitive power which is vaguely Platonic, an apprehension of the mysteries which move behind the phenomenological world. His artist-heroes always display a perception of the "ghostly paradigm of things" upon which Nature, in Yeats' poem, "plays" in a "spume." Shade expresses this idea here:

> How fully I felt nature glued to me
> And how my childish palate loved the taste
> Half-fish, half-honey, of that golden paste!
>
> My picture book was at an early age
> The painted parchment papering our cage:
> Mauve rings around the moon; blood-orange sun;
> Twinned Iris; and that rare phenomenon
> The iridule—when, beautiful and strange,
> In a bright sky above a mountain range
> One opal cloudlet in an oval form
> Reflects the rainbow of a thunderstorm
> Which in a distant valley has been staged—
> For we are most artistically caged.   [Canto One, 11.102–114]

The "iridule" (Nabokov's coinage: Iris is the goddess of rainbows) is evidently a partial analogue of art's mediation between our world and the world which is available to us only momentarily, imperfectly, the world beyond the cage of time and

death, the *"abstruse,/Unfinished poem"* to which our life is a
commentary (and perhaps as different from its real design as
Kinbote's commentary is from Shade's unfinished poem). *"Life
is a message scribbled in the dark,"* Shade writes, a statement
that at least implies a scribbler, even if it also signifies a certain
indecipherability. Logic isn't much help, but that in itself
shouldn't discourage belief that there is a designer and a design:

> . . . *if* prior to life we had
> Been able to imagine life, what mad,
> Impossible, unutterably weird,
> Wonderful nonsense it might have appeared!
>
> So why join in the vulgar laughter? Why
> Scorn a hereafter none can verify:
> The Turk's delight, the future lyres, the talks
> With Socrates and Proust in cypress walks,
> The seraph with his six flamingo wings,
> And Flemish hells with porcupines and things?
> It isn't that we dream too wild a dream:
> The trouble is we do not make it seem
> Sufficiently unlikely.   [Canto Two, 11.217–229]

The Voices of *Pale Fire:* Shade and His Poem

We are interested in Nabokov less perhaps for his mimicry and
characterization than for his voice—the prose, the interests, the
predilections, the feelings expressed or implied which go into that
ineffable presence within a novel which we call a voice, and
which forms its irreducible identity. The voice of a novel is its
nervous system—its complex sensitivity extending both within
and without itself; like all nervous systems, it is infinitely complex
and ultimately mysterious. It is the source of a novel's most
subtle fascination and appeal. A novelist's voice involves his relationship with the material and his relationship with the reader.

It is hard to think of any other writer with a voice as distinctive as Nabokov's. But here, as with the moral aspects of his fiction, his limitations have been largely ignored. For all his powers of language and imagery, Nabokov is simply not free. Even art that is "fantastically deceitful and complex" is not really to be equated with freedom, and if we listen carefully to his use of voice and voices, we discover the concerns to which Nabokov always returns and the boundaries beyond which he will not go. It is useful to at least start with the generality that Nabokov's fiction is a precondition for the use of Nabokov's voice—that passionate, hyperbolic, worldly, elegant, narcissistic, venomous, hilarious carnival, which, in Martin Green's words, "so energetically avoids every suspicion of the ordinary, of the obvious, of the morally or intellectually banal."[6]

Nabokov usually chooses from among three options in order to realize the greatest range of possibilities for his voice. He will erase the difference between first and third person by creating an authorial equivalent with a voice identical to his own. *Bend Sinister* and *The Gift* are examples, as is, on a smaller scale, "Spring in Fialta." If he creates a character who has no possibility of possessing that voice, then the tale surrounding that character is endowed with a Nabokovian overvoice. Examples of this choice are *Pnin* and an early novel, *King, Queen, Knave.* His last option is, I think, simultaneously the most desirable and the most difficult for him, and that is a voice of first-person narration. The novels *Despair, The Eye, The Real Life of Sebastian Knight,* and *Lolita* are examples of first-person narration, and so is *Pale Fire,* although there the choice is modified.

Each of these options involves advantages and limitations. If the overvoice and the protagonist share a voice, they are almost the same sort of "people," and we have seen that Nabokov will allow his alter egos a very limited range of dramatic possibilities

—they have no interest in society or in its judgment; their genius assures their careers; they are not jealous or ambitious in the ordinary sense. Any woman that his favorite could marry (for example, Zina Mertz in *The Gift,* Sybil Shade in *Pale Fire,* Ada Veen) is as different from the rest of the milieu as, say, Cordelia is from her sisters, and instantly recognizes the pricelessness of the protagonist. There is, then, very little possibility of generating dramatic involvement out of the protagonist's desires or career. Since voice is not a novelist's sole concern, although we may claim for the moment that it is his most important, the creation of a central character who has the same voice as Nabokov will then divide the fiction either into an exercise in pure voice, with very little plot activity and no dramatic tension, like *The Gift;* or into a fiction which has a strong melodramatic or exterior tension, but in which the equivalent is only a passive agent, as in *Bend Sinister* and *Invitation to a Beheading.*

Pale Fire is a hybrid in this respect. Nabokov's voice and Shade's, if superimposed, would match almost perfectly—in fact, in his *Playboy* interview Nabokov quoted from memory these lines from Shade without any qualification as to their judgment:

> Now I shall speak of evil as none has
> Spoken before. I loathe such things as jazz;
> The white-hosed moron torturing a black
> Bull, rayed with red; abstractist bric-a-brac;
> Primitivist folk-masks; progressive schools;
> Music in supermarkets; swimming pools;
> Brutes, bores, class-conscious Philistines, Freud, Marx,
> Fake thinkers, puffed-up poets, frauds and sharks.
>
> [Canto Four, 11.923–930]

Nabokov uses Shade's voice for speculation, metaphysics, and poetry, just as he had used Fyodor's in *The Gift.* We listen to it dealing with his daughter's death, creating poetry, coming to terms with death and life after death—but these are not dramatic problems, and no plot can embody them.

Once we understand the importance of Nabokov's intimacy with his favorites, it is easy to understand why he cannot bear Eliot's poetry: "I read [Eliot and Pound] . . . in the guest room of an American friend's house, and not only remained completely indifferent to them but could not understand why anybody should bother about them."[7] Nabokov is obviously not the kind of man who could stand for a moment Eliot's Anglican dogma or concern with social disintegration, and Nabokov's resistance extends to Eliot's theory of impersonal creation and his failure to insist on the primacy of the artist.

Eliot's poetic technique is translational: the images habitually illustrate meaning for the idea, emotion, or theme to which they are yoked. This is part of the famous "objective correlative" passage in Eliot's remarks on *Hamlet,* and Eliot's poetic practice is to vivify his emotional meanings by translating these meanings into other sorts of energy-units: he claims that the words and the meaning bear a mechanical but mysterious relationship to each other—neither more nor less mechanical and mysterious than the relationship between quartz crystals and radio waves, or "carbon, sunlight, and blind throbbings" to biological life. Those images, phrases, or chains of events which necessarily "terminate in sensory experience" all ultimately translate emotion, convey it, make it accessible: we are, after all, surrounded by radio waves, but in order to be accessible to us, they must be translated by a humble mechanical affair. The role of this humble mechanism is precisely that which Eliot habitually attributes to the poet. Eliot insists that the artist is only a *medium,* and goes so far as to completely segregate the man from the artist: "Experiences which are important for the man may take no place in the poetry, and those which become important in the poetry may play quite a negligible part in the man, the personality"; even more strikingly, Eliot can call the artistic process "a continual self-sacrifice, a continual extinction of personality,"[8] which is about as far from Nabokov (and Shade) as we can get.

One of Eliot's poetic personae lost a daughter, too; and the expression of the grief and the tentative hope of regaining the lost child are expressed in "Marina."[9] The speaker is Pericles, or at least Pericles is part of the impersonation. But the voice includes much more than could possibly inhere in the scrupulous impersonation of a simple dramatic monologue:

> . . . and the woodthrush singing through the fog
> What images return
> O my daughter.
> Those who sharpen the tooth of the dog, meaning
> Death
> Those who glitter with the glory of the hummingbird, meaning
> Death
> Those who sit in the sty of contentment, meaning
> Death
> Those who suffer the ecstasy of animals, meaning
> Death
> Are become unsubstantial, reduced by a wind.

The specific daughter, and the unique and personal grief, are translated by the larger and more comprehensive voice into that series of general statements: "meaning Death;" meaning, in fact, Christian damnation, a general proposition. The verse is, in the truest sense, a *medium:* the specific particulars are always taking on larger meanings, and the larger meanings search out their expression in the specific.

Just enough of the specific and local is supplied to make the situation an actuality, but the intentions of the poem extend beyond this local situation and the emotions of a specific, single-voiced father, and beyond his experience of grief, death, and regeneration.

In contrast, Shade's couplets indicate different intentions and a different idea of art's uses and possibilities. Notice the specificity of the Shadean hereafter in this passage, and notice also that the couplet rhyme tends to reinforce a surety of feeling and a specificity of meaning:

> I'm ready to become a floweret
> Or a fat fly, but never, to forget.
> And I'll turn down eternity unless
> The melancholy and the tenderness
> Of mortal life; the passion and the pain;
> The claret taillight of that dwindling plane
> Off Hesperus; your gesture of dismay
> On running out of cigarettes; the way
> You smile at dogs; the trail of silver slime
> Snails leave on flagstones; this good ink, this rhyme,
> This index card, this slender rubber band
> Which always forms, when dropped, an ampersand,
> Are found in Heaven by the newlydead.
>
> [Canto Three, 11.523–535]

Implicit in this vision of the importance of things in their unique thingness is an insistence that no exterior scheme be applied to them. Shade's practice, then, is *terminal* rather than translational; and so, indeed, is Nabokov's: "The use of symbols [is] hateful because it substitutes a dead general idea for a live specific impression. . . . In high art and pure science detail is everything."[10]

Shade's lost daughter, in contrast to the daughter of Eliot's Pericles, has a definite personality and a definite psychology—even a pathology. Hazel suffers horribly from her own physical ugliness; Shade, genetically responsible for it, as well as for her brilliance, suffers with her. There will be no "old Pan" interested in Hazel, and although "Virgins have written some *resplendent* books," Hazel's personality becomes morbid and destructive out of self-loathing and shame and loneliness:

> . . . She'd criticize
> Ferociously our projects, and with eyes
> Expressionless sit on her tumbled bed
> Spreading her swollen feet, scratching her head
> With psoriatic fingernails, and moan,
> Murmuring dreadful words in monotone.
>
> [Canto Two, 11.351–356]

But aside from her physical ugliness, we find again that turn of mind and personality and the feelings for life and death with which Nabokov always endows his mad young suicides and fantasts. "She had strange fears, strange fantasies, strange force/Of character," Shade claims; she is fascinated in a certain psychokinetic phenomenon that takes place in the barn of a farmer who hanged himself; she wins prizes in French and history; and, like virtually all of Nabokov's favorites, she feels words are there to be looked at as well as through: "She twisted words: pot, top, / Spider, redips. And 'powder' was 'red wop'" (Canto Two, 11. 344–345, 347–348).

Nabokov's destructive machinery has been set up, and we now find, as we always find, the reel slowing down as death approaches the favorite and those whom Nabokov and the favorite love.

Shade's technique is to present her suicide dramatically, with Hazel, deserted by her blind date, finding for herself an icy New England lake in which to drown. Speaking couplets from the vantage point of time, and following Hazel in imagination, Shade does not find in his daughter's death any general significance, none of the exquisite, indefinite beauty and hope we find in "Marina," but his involvement with his own dead daughter and his hopes for her survival are a matter of specifics; he will "resign" nothing, retain everything. The gallows-walk itself, so carefully contrived and ornamented for our participation, would have no significance if the loss was not going to be real—a loss of the world of specifies: the claret taillight; snailslime; the rubber band turned literary by its long association with index cards.

It is interesting to know that although Nabokov cannot stand Eliot's poetry, he likes the John Crowe Ransom poem "Bells for John Whiteside's Daughter."[11] The reason may well lie not so much with the obvious parallel dramatic situation—for the Eliot poem shares it—as with Ransom's success in smuggling into his poem full-blown, potentially mawkish feelings, and yet making the poem work. In the Ranson poem, the most vivid image is that of the little girl harrying the geese across the lawn. The image's effect is subtle and complex. It is comic, but the comedy inheres less in the little girl than in the "sleepy and proud" geese, and the geese are only partially played for comedy, for they give back to the poem and lovely image of themselves "like a snow cloud / Dripping their snow on the green grass."[12] Further, these vexed, beautiful, comical geese, while crying "in goose, Alas," contribute that shimmering but almost unforgivable word "Alas" to the poem, and although they regret her "tireless heart" only because it disturbs their gooselike "noon apple-dreams," the "tireless heart" is thus smuggled in as a statement which we, as non-geese know to be a pitiful irony. Just as with Nabokov's vision of the swan, and his alliance of it with Mademoiselle only after he brings it under control as a "dodo-like creature," so Ransom's immortal geese, retaining both a fairytale beauty and yet convincingly visualized as "lazy" and comical, contribute to the poem a means by which its emotional effect can be dilated without being sentimentally compromised.

The quaint, laconic terms with which death is described—the "brown study" that is repeated twice and the inanimate "primly propped"—represent strategic withdrawals at the points in the poem where we would expect elegy or eulogy. The real emotional life of the poem, however, lies with the vivid, comical, beautiful "war" between the geese that "scuttle" and the single-minded, "tireless" little girl who makes them scuttle; and death, about which we suddenly realize we can say nothing except that it will include no goose-chasing, no "speed," no orchard, and which is indifferent to the notion that any heart can be "tireless." That death resides wholly in the "brown study" and especially in the small, ugly, and wholly inanimate "propped" that ends the poem.

Ransom's method is thus indirect, but not translational or mediational. Grief is quite localized, emotion is vivid and particular, and the death is that of a little girl and nothing more: all the meanings of the poem are exhausted with its singular emotional meaning.

The death of Shade's daughter, his guesses about an afterlife, the possibilities of art, form the major themes of the poem "Pale Fire"; it remains for the last canto to achieve a certain sense of completion, if not of resolution, and Shade achieves it easily enough—the completion of the poem resembles the completion of the summer day and, in a further sense, the completion of all the possibilities within his own consciousness, the completion of his life. Nabokov, who above all verisimilitude desires the esthetic effect of closure, arranges for Shade's extinction.

> Gently the day has passed in a sustained
> Low hum of harmony. The brain is drained
> And a brown ament, and the noun I meant
> To use but did not, dry on the cement.

Maybe my sensual love for the *consonne*
D'appui, Echo's fey child, is based upon
A feeling of fantastically planned,
Richly rhymed life. [Canto Four, 11.963–970]

Here it is especially apparent that the use of the couplets, with their closure, surety, and sense of completeness, underscores that sense of control, frequently visible control, which Nabokov's work always gives. The art itself, the couplets, reinforce the statement that Shade's life is "fantastically planned,/Richly rhymed," and a few minutes after he writes these final lines, Kinbote calls upon him, and they both go toward Judge Goldsworth's house, sublet to Kinbote by interested fates, where Shade is destroyed by Gradus-Grey. The plan and rhyme thus extend both into and out of Shade's poem, for the completion of the poem signifies and makes necessary the completion of the life. All of Shade has been dramatically exhausted, and his voice in the poem is used up (Kinbote and Nabokov can of course play back any bits that they need to in the Commentary). The art within the poem is met and completed by the life outside the poem. In *Bend Sinister,* there is also a two-level exchange, but in that novel the fictional level of Krug and Paduk is met and completed from above by another level of consciousness, that of the artist. Nabokov's worlds are not only double, they are superimposed, and they penetrate each other with extraordinarily complex effects. One of these effects in *Pale Fire* is to reinforce Shade's claim that there is something behind "the scene" that plans for us. After all, it planned for him.

Kinbote's Voice

Since most of the novel is related to us by Kinbote (or Botkin, or Charles the Beloved), much of the success or failure of the book must lie with his performance.

Judging *Pale Fire* by Nabokov's other achievements, especially by *Pnin* and *Lolita*, I find *Pale Fire* the least satisfying, the least enjoyable of the three. The reasons have nothing to do with the intricacy of the planes of reality and illusion and deception or the extraordinary artificiality of the novel. Even if I do not agree with Mary McCarthy's ecstatic judgment of *Pale Fire* as "a creation of perfect beauty, symmetry, strangeness, originality, and moral truth,"[13] I believe she is correct in pointing out that one of the novel's most striking features is its moral, compassionate, and humane interest in Shade and, curiously enough, in Kinbote. "Love is the burden of *Pale Fire*, love and loss," she states, and this statement is true of all of Nabokov's work. But the novel's relative failure seems to me to lie with the choice of Kinbote to tell the tale, and with the moral and esthetic effect that this choice, coupled with Nabokov's predilections, has on the voice and structure of the novel.

Kinbote can of course be unintentionally funny, when we see beyond or around his fantastic and bizarre egocentrism: "[Shade's] laconic suggestion [at the faculty club] that I 'try the pork' amused me. I am a strict vegetarian, and I like to cook my own meals. Consuming something that had been handled by a fellow creature was, I explained to the rubicund convives, as repulsive to me as eating any creature, and that would include— lowering my voice— the pulpous, pony-tailed girl student who served us and licked her pencil" (20).

He is quite funny in his homosexuality, his pedantry, his egocentricity; and we understand perfectly well what attitude we are to take with this bizarre academician who can speak dreamily of a "moody, delicate, rather wonderful boy", which is foolish and rather pitiable but at least affectionately tender, but can dismiss the entire synchronous arrangement of Shade's counterpoint between Hazel's suicide and her parents' night at home with the

TV as "too labored and long, especially since the synchronization device has been already worked to death by Flaubert and Joyce. Otherwise the pattern is exquisite" (196). And we know with whom we are dealing when we hear Kinbote blandly comment on Shade's portrayal of his daughter: "True, in this canto [Shade] has unburdened himself pretty thoroughly, and his picture of Hazel is quite clear and complete; maybe a little too complete, architectonically, since the reader cannot help feeling that it has been expanded and elaborated to the detriment of certain other richer and rarer matters ousted by it. But a commentator's obligations cannot be shirked, however dull the information he must collect and convey" (164).

The characterization is ripe with such overdelicacies as Kinbote's syrupy evocation of an adolescent partner: "When stripped and shiny in the midst of the bath house, his bold virilia contrasted harshly with his girlish grace. He was a regular faunlet" (123). By such self-indictment Kinbote is allowed to depict himself, and we are amused by the performance and know exactly what we are to make of him. The homosexuality, always an aspect of sterility and monstrosity in Nabokov's world, is kept allusive and indirect; and Kinbote's tenderness, even if silly, is never nasty, and we are not required to condemn it or loathe him for it.

But Nabokov also presents us with aspects of Kinbote that do not successfully fuse with the pederast and pedant. Along with his strictly comic creation—which requires consistent exaggeration—he has tried to give us aspects of an authorial favorite again. The mimicry is forfeited by this enlargement, for Nabokov has made, I think, an imperfect match of voice and feeling, and the effect is blurry and troublesome.

Kinbote loves Shade and Shade's poetry. This love immediately removes him from the realm of total monsterhood, since it is clearly a moral and esthetic positive. Kinbote's political conservatism could also be Shade's or his creator's. Relating an incident concerning his own "identity" as the king of Zembla, Kinbote recalls that in a faculty club discussion of the Zemblan Revolution one of the opinions about the fate of the exiled monarch was put forth by a certain "professor of physics." Just as in *Bend Sinister*, Nabokov has seized the scruff of a supernumerary in order to get in a few lines of opinion—in this case, anti-Leftist sentiment: "A professor of physics now joined in. He was a so-called Pink, who believed in what so-called Pinks believe in (Progressive Education, the Integrity of anyone spying for Russia, Fall-outs occasioned solely by US-made bombs, the existence in the near past of a McCarthy Era, Soviet achievements including *Dr. Zhivago,* and so forth)" (266).

This is a list of indictments that Nabokov, not Kinbote, has prepared. We find Shade condemning progressive education in his poem, and the favorite Humbert Humbert drawing a bead on it. The "McCarthy era" concern is used by Nabokov as a mildy unfavorable clue to academic character; for example, when Pnin gives his little party at Waindell and Dr. Hagen arrives with a bottle of vodka, a certain guest, Dr. Thomas, "places" himself for us when he cracks, "I hope the Senator did not see you walking about with that stuff" (155). Herbert Gold recalls arriving at Cornell to teach and having Nabokov offer him his annotated copy of *Dr. Zhivago,* "which he called 'Dr. Van Cliburn.' "[14] And Nabokov can be quite savage about, say, Bertrand Russell's organizing a demonstration against nuclear arms while in Russia, in "Tomsk or Atomsk," the Soviets plan to vaporize the Western democracies in a mushroom cloud. Kinbote's Pink list is, moreover, not really the list of a royalist—and a deposed and exiled king is nothing if not a royalist; it is drawn up from the point of view of an American conservative and anticommunist. At least progressive education, fallouts, the Rosenberg case, McCarthy, and the fatuous worship of *Dr. Zhivago* among the literary set are not mentioned elsewhere as Zemblan social problems. The voice is Nabokov's own, and the characterization suffers from being preempted in this manner.

The use of Kinbote as a moral agent alters his voice and makes it difficult for the reader to arrive at a clear idea of his character. Kinbote must pass judgment on Gradus, and in passing this judgment Kinbote and Shade are ethically and esthetically united in the reader's mind *against* Gradus, and the difference between the poet and the commentator becomes insignificant when compared to the difference between both of them and the horrifying little subhuman inching closer and closer. Both Shade and Kinbote can "cheerfully deride / The dedicated imbeciles" (Canto 3, 11. 607–608) who carry out political assassinations, and Kinbote reveals his humanistic streak when he offers us the "anti-Darwinian" aphorism: "The one who kills is *always* his victim's inferior" (234). Further, Kinbote's lush homosexuality is positively healthy when compared to Gradus' brief sexual career: "Sexual impulses had greatly bothered [Gradus] at one time but that was over. After his wife, a beader in Radugovitra, had left him (with a gypsy lover), he had lived in sin with his mother-in-law until she was removed, blind and dropsical, to an asylum for decayed widows. Since then he had tried several times to castrate himself, had been laid up at the Glassman Hospital with a severe infection, and now, at forty-four, was quite cured of the lust that Nature, the grand cheat, puts into us to inveigle us into propagation" (253).

This passage not only makes Gradus a monster, it also lends to the commentator the *opposite* values, and the opposite values in relation to Gradus can only be positive, nonmonstrous. Thus, the presence of Gradus causes Kinbote to undergo an evolution, toward Shade and toward Nabokov. Notice the return by Nabokov to the condemnation of the "general idea," and how indifferently this condemnation is "smuggled" into Kinbote's indictment of Gradus:

[Gradus] disliked injustice and deception. He disliked their union—they were always together—with a wooden passion that neither had, nor needed, words to express itself. Such a dislike should have deserved praise had it not been a by-product of the man's hopeless stupidity. He called unjust and deceitful everything that surpassed his understanding. He worshiped general ideas and did so with a pedantic aplomb. The generality was godly, the specific diabolical. . . . People who knew too much, scientists, writers, mathmaticians, crystalographers and so forth, were no better than kings or priests: they all held an unfair share of power of which others were cheated. A plain decent fellow should constantly be on the watch for some piece of clever knavery on the part of nature and neighbor. [152]

Kinbote's voice is limited, and it is the dearth of possibilities open to it which we feel when we compare it to the voices of Humbert Humbert, of Nabokov himself in *Speak, Memory,* or that combinational voice—sometimes omniscient, sometimes Fyodor's—that we hear in *The Gift.* Kinbote is not a great artist, not sane, not sexually healthy, not able to love; he is disqualified from the highest achievements of voice of which Nabokov is capable. The author must play Kinbote as consistently and self-consciously secondary to Shade, and this diminishment truncates the possibilities open to him—the interests he can have and the prose in which he can express them. Under the burden of maintaining the characterization, Nabokov cannot give to this monster's voice the range of interest, ecstasy, wit, and comedy that he himself exhibits in *Speak, Memory,* or that Humbert Humbert, a more nearly perfect monster, exhibits in *Lolita.*

Kinbote can have no tenderness or curiosity that is not distorted by monstrosity and egocentricity, and yet it is "curiosity, tenderness, kindness and ecstasy" which Nabokov attributes to that mode of consciousness, "aesthetic bliss," which he feels to be his art's highest achievement and sole justification. We cannot even begin to have passages from Kinbote like this one from Nabokov's *Speak, Memory,* just as the tender passages in Shade's poem will remain only beautiful *language* to the scholar-monster:

You [my wife] remember the discoveries we made (supposedly made by all parents) : the perfect shape of [our baby's] miniature finger-nails, of the hand you silently showed me as it lay, stranded starfish-wise, on your palm; the epidermic texture of limb and cheek, to which attention was drawn in dimmed, faraway tones, as if the soft-ness of touch could be rendered only by the softness of distance; that swimming, sloping, elusive something about the dark-bluish tint of the iris which seemed still to retain the shadows it had absorbed of ancient, fabulous forests where there were more birds than tigers and more fruit than thorns, and where, in some dappled depth, man's mind has been born; and, above all, an infant's first journey into the next dimension, the newly established nexus between eye and reachable object, which the career boys in biometrics or in the rat-maze racket think they can explain. It occurs to me that the closest reproduction of the mind's birth obtainable is the stab of wonder that accompanies the precise moment when, gazing at a tangle of twigs and leaves, one suddenly realizes that what had seemed a natural component of that tangle is a marvelously dis-guised insect or bird.[15]

The sharp visual beauty of the passage and the alliance of its tone with everything life-giving are, by definition, beyond Kin-bote's powers. The tenderness is not adulterated with perversion, the intelligence is unclouded by egocentricity.

Shade perceives, or hopes he does, a deliberate design in life, an esthetic pattern, a "sense behind the scene." In a mad way

Kinbote perceives a pattern, too: he gazes at a seeming "tangle," and suddenly perceives something hidden within. Shade dead, Kinbote clutches the shade of Shade, the (literally) immortal poem. At first reading he is outraged. "I sped through it, snarling, as a furious young heir through an old deceiver's testament. . . . Where was Zembla the Fair?" (296). The art is empty for him; there is no "sense behind scene." Then a curious, predictable, and almost salutary phenomenon occurs. The poem, stretching across his own distorted conceptions, starts to take on different contours:

> Gradually I regained my usual composure. I reread *Pale Fire* more carefully. I liked it better when expecting less. And what was that? What was that dim distant music, those vestiges of color in the air? Here and there I discovered in it and especially, especially in the invaluable variants, echoes and spangles of my mind, a long ripplewake of my glory. I now felt a new, pitiful tenderness toward the poem as one has for a fickle young creature who has been stolen and brutally enjoyed by a black giant but now again is safe in our hall and park, whistling with the stableboys, swimming with the tame seal. The spot still hurts, it must hurt, but with strange gratitude we kiss those heavy wet eyelids and caress that polluted flesh. [297]

And so the solipsistic process continues with its new raw material. Nothing is indigestible to Kinbote's ravenous obsession: thus the Commentary. But there is a tinge of triumph in Kinbote's madness. Shade realizes that it should be viewed as a subjective accommodation to life's brutality rather than as a lunatic's masquerade. Kinbote overhears the poet explaining the distinction to his hostess at a cocktail party (although he fails to recognize that it is his madness Shade is sympathizing with). " 'That [madness] is the wrong word' [Shade] said. 'One should not apply it to a person who deliberately peels off a drab and unhappy past and replaces it with a brilliant invention. That's merely turning a new leaf with the left hand' " (238).

But Kinbote's solipsism, the egocentricity Nabokov has fitted him with, draws everything toward itself and seems to squander its energy in impersonation. The "ripplewake" that Kinbote suddenly begins to perceive in Shade's poem is embodied in a metaphor of lush homosexuality, for Nabokov is beholden to his characterization, and Kinbote's perversity circumscribes the possibilities open to his voice. There is only room for a little digression about Proust (Nabokov's fidelity to the characterization is evidenced by the fact that Gide and Cocteau, two more homosexuals, are the other modern writers Kinbote mentions most frequently), some brittle academic shoptalk, and other minor matters. But Kinbote's voice is incapable of the kind of fully conscious tenderness, curiosity, and ecstasy, and even the gentle fun, of the voice of *Speak, Memory,* or the voice of Humbert Humbert.

As I shall try to explain in a discussion of *Lolita,* the use of the monster Humbert Humbert to tell the story at last allows a fusion of the highest possibilities of voice with plot activity that is generated out of the narrator's own personality. We have seen how difficult it is for Nabokov to achieve both full voice and meaningful plot in a tale about one of his favorites. His feelings toward his favorites and his indifference to the novelistic middle ground, the usual forms of human affairs that occupy most of our novelists most of the time, combine to polarize his fiction toward the extremes of *The Gift* or *Bend Sinister,* toward pure voice or melodrama. Either of these alternatives is in some measure undesirable, or at least neither makes full use of Nabokov's greatest gifts.

Pale Fire seems strategically less sound than *Pnin* and *Lolita,* and this weakness is at least partially a result of Nabokov's failure to fuse, somehow, voice with favorite. Kinbote can have only a monster's croak; Shade, exhausting his effects in his "own" poem, does not really fit into the frame of the narrative. In his poem "The Room," Nabokov says,

> A poet's death is, after all,
> a question of technique, a neat
> enjambment, a melodic fall.

This is a fitting description of Shade's death—his artful, painless departure from a novel in which he has never functioned adequately as a character. *Pnin* and *Lolita,* surer in their narrative techniques because Nabokov has chosen more cautiously from among his options, achieve a better synthesis of voice and activity than does *Pale Fire.*

4

Pnin

Pnin and Liza

Although Nabokov told Alfred Appel that the whole design of *Pnin* was complete in his imagination before parts of it began appearing in *The New Yorker*,[1] in its final form the work seems in many ways to be more a series of sketches than a novel. The sketches show Timofey Pnin, serially offered to us as addlepated "assistant professor *emeritus*," émigré, deserted husband, substitute "water father" to his wife's son Victor, campus joke, scarred survivor of the twentieth century. Of the novels Nabokov has written since his emigration to America in 1940 (and his return to Europe in 1959), *Pnin* is the least fantastic, the most realistic. It involves no madness, is without melodrama, and does not employ its own artifice as its own primary subject. Unlike *Bend Sinister*, it lacks the horror of a police state. It lacks the eroticism of *Lolita*. It also lacks the major irony of Kinbotian madness that is part of the mechanism of *Pale Fire*. And unlike *Ada*, it does not depend on an unusual conception of earth-space-time. It is easily the most gentle and humane of all Nabokov's novels.

In place of a conventional plot, Nabokov has substituted a series of relatively unconnected incidents, the first of which is Pnin's trip as lecturer to an upstate campus at Cremona. After various bungles on train and bus, he suffers a spell in which the past revisits him, and the segment ends with a vision, while he is onstage, of his dead beloved family and sweetheart. Another segment traces Pnin's involvement with Liza Wind, a vicious, but beautiful émigré poetess and psychoanalyst to whom he was briefly married. Incidents in their relationship appear elsewhere. Pnin makes a brief stay with other Russian émigrés at a friend's retreat, and his stay culminates in his vision of Mira Belochkin destroyed at Buchenwald. Victor Wind at the exclusive New England prep school, St. Bart's, forms a segment, and Nabokov adds a passage on the school's resident artist, Lake. Pnin gives a housewarming party; and the novel's last segment deals with the relationship of a now fully materialized first-person narrator, roughly Nabokov himself, with the Pnin who has lost his job at Waindell just as the narrator accepts a position there: Pnin leaves on his birthday without speaking to the narrator—he has urgent psychic reasons for not doing so—and we last see him at the wheel of his car, leaving Waindell forever.

All of these incidents, and many others less substantial, are told by an overvoice that evokes the past. It is usually the European past, frequently the Russian one, "a brilliant cosmos that seemed all the fresher for having been abolished by one blow of history" (12), so that the narrative is neither physically nor temporally confined, and in this respect resembles consciousness itself. The novel includes much more than any catalogue of its incidents could suggest, for the present is always yielding up the past, the past is always and immediately at hand. Pnin's past is fiercely and even dangerously real and alive to him. Although he is not an equivalent for Nabokov—he could not have written *Lolita* as Humbert Humbert did, could not be the world-celebrated philosopher Krug is, nor enjoy the coterie reputation that John Shade or Sebastian Knight achieve—he has a great many of the primary Nabokovian positive traits: he loves Gogol, Pushkin, and

Shakespeare, and is disgusted by the Soviet Communists; he does not believe in Liza's Freudian or Jungian theories; he has insomnia and a bad heart; he is uxorious and utterly loving, but is captivated by a woman unworthy of him, as are Humbert and Krug and the narrator of "Spring in Fialta," Albinus Kretschmar in *Laughter in the Dark*, and Cincinnatus in *Invitation to a Beheading*; and he has no social or career ambitions, except to be left alone to research and write his *petite histoire* of Russian culture.

But these positive traits are the sources of admiration and appeal for what is essentially a comical, if ultimately tragicomical, creation, for we are also invited *outside* to join the narrator in seeing Pnin from a comic vantage. We are shown a Pnin who is "inept with his hands to a rare degree. . . . The devoutly plugged-in clock would make nonsense of his mornings after a storm in the middle of the night had paralyzed the local power station. The frame of his spectacles would snap in mid-bridge, leaving him with two identical pieces, which he would vaguely attempt to unite, in the hope, perhaps, of some organic marvel of restoration coming to the rescue. The zipper a gentleman depends on most would come loose in his puzzled hand at some nightmare moment of haste and despair" (14).

And of course his long and hopeless pursuit of the English language is comical, but comical in a harmless way. Humbert, Kinbote, or Van Veen have talons and tails; Pnin is a *naif* and a butt, and clearly contains some of the elements of which Kinbote is made—pedantry, a demonic linguistic and literary fixation, an exile's nostalgia, a certain amount of bad temper, a reverence for real poetry, a hatred of Marx and Freud. But Pnin is the least monstrous of human beings. Nabokov makes the non-Kinbote side of Pnin vivid and moving through the little scholar's memory of Mira Belochkin, and his relationship with Victor and with Victor's mother, Liza Bogolepov Pnin Wind.

Liza is a version of the Nina we met in "Spring in Fialta" in that she is a clever fake and her life is full of "gibberish" and "lies", but she is a far more vicious version; unlike Nina, Liza is actively ambitious, callous, and vain. Even more unlike Nina, she is cruel. She is a bad poetess. Worse, she is a psychiatrist. It is difficult to express the disgust that Nabokov feels for the psychiatrist or for anything connected with Freud. In his *Playboy* interview, Nabokov himself made the effort: "The ordeal [of being psychoanalyzed] is much too silly and disgusting to be contemplated even as a joke. Freudism and all it has tainted with its grotesque implications and methods, appear to me to be one of the vilest deceits practiced by people on themselves and on others. I reject it utterly, along with a few other medieval items still adored by the ignorant, the conventional, or the very sick.[2]

Pnin loves Liza inordinately, magically, with no reference to her personality. But Nabokov, who cannot let his beloved Pnin be impressed by Liza's *pishooslinie* ("psychoasinie") interests, allows him to feel only "revulsion and pity" for her projects.

In 1940, pregnant Liza (the fetus is Victor, the father Eric Wind) uses Pnin, whom she has only recently abandoned, to supply the necessary visa requirements for her own emigration from Paris to America, and Pnin finds that Liza's lover and colleague, Eric Wind, a German psychiatrist, has accompanied them to America on the same ship. Although he has been horribly humiliated, Pnin is still very much in love with Liza, and we are assured that he would still readily give her his life "with the wet stems cut and a bit of fern, and all of it wrapped up as crisply as at the earth-smelling florist's when the rain makes grey and green mirrors of Easter day" (46). Years later, when Victor is enrolled at exclusive St. Bart's, Liza thinks nothing of visiting Pnin at Waindell College to ask him to contribute to the expense, and she chattily relates to him a few tidbits about her latest affair. After a stay of only hours, she returns to Eric—for they still keep a tenuous connection in order to give Victor what they claim is the Oedipal triangle so necessary to a young male's psychic growth. "[Pnin] saw her off, and walked back through the park. To hold her, to keep her—just as she was—with her cruelty, with her vulgarity, with her blinding blue eyes, with her miserable poetry, with her fat feet, with her impure, dry, sordid, infantile soul. All of a sudden he thought: If people are reunited in Heaven (I don't believe it, but suppose), then how shall I stop it from creeping upon me, over me, that shriveled, helpless, lame thing, her soul?" (57–58).

It is important to notice that, since Pnin is capable of judging Liza realistically, which is necessarily to judge her harshly, the bond that holds him true to her is inexplicable. No matter how skillfully Nabokov conceals these magical psychic givens—the suicide triangle in "Triangle within Circle," Kinbote's homosexuality, even Humbert's nympholepsy are other examples—his dependence on our accepting them at face value is in itself an indication of the way he writes and the way we should read. The force of Pnin's feelings—his love of Liza, against all judgment, intelligence, taste, and common sense—is simply and unaccountably magical. It is absolute. It is once-and-for-all. But it is also illogical and dangerous. It is, then, part of the world of the fairytale. Vasili's cloud, castle, and lake; the narrator's love for Nina in "Spring in Fialta"; Luzhin's madness; Cincinnatus' imprisonment and pending execution—everywhere in Nabokov we find the same use of the magical given, and this in turn implies what we usually *fail* to find in Nabokov: indications of any interest in moral development, in change, choice, in the process of learning.

Nabokov's fiction usually offers us a set of poised relationships and situations, wound up to release their energy with maximum force, for maximum emotional effect. But the way in which the psychological mechanism has been constructed and the way in which all the moving parts have been joined together will not bear close scrutiny if we approach it expecting psychological realism. At some point in any piece of Nabokov's fiction the reader must accept a bond of fairytale potency and mysteriousness.

Liza Wind is thus the Dark Lady, la belle dame sans merci, the vamp, and represents the destructive, fatally erotic type of Nabokovian female. Although Nabokov has made no attempt to balance the types in this novel, Joan Clements appears in it as the clearly realized incarnation of the other primary Nabokovian female, the Ideal Faculty Wife: brisk, pleasant, intelligent, commonsensical, fun, compassionate—just the kind of woman Krug's Olga is, the kind we might visualize as the narrator's wife in "Spring in Fialta," and just the type of woman John Shade feels his wife to be. It is usually the fate of Nabokov's protagonists to be involved with these Dark Ladies at some point, and of all his protagonists, Pnin is surely the most helplessly ensnared.

Liza Wind's psychiatric career allows Nabokov to embody within her character many of the negative elements which are part of the novel's ethical and moral structure. Liza herself stands for a great deal that Nabokov loathes: ambition, fakery, Freud, philistinism, total indifference to the privacy of others. Moreover, she and her husband and psychiatric colleague, Eric Wind, are both champions of the *group*.

In its polarity of good characters and evil characters the novel makes, as does *Bend Sinister,* a distinction between the individual and the group as one of its primary ethical terms. Although this division is not as sensational as that between Krug and the

Ekwilists, Vasili and the Pleasantrip crowd, or Shade and Gradus, it is one of the most important modes of judgment that we are offered. Liza and Eric are wholly of the group; Pnin is quite otherwise:

Incidentally it was deadening to hear [Eric] and Liza smacking their lips over the word "group." In a long letter to distressed Pnin, Professor Chateau affirmed that Dr. Wind even called Siamese twins "a group." And indeed progressive, idealistic Wind dreamed of a happy world consisting of Siamese centuplets, anatomically conjoined communities, whole nations built around a communicating liver. "It is nothing but a kind of microcosmos of communism—all that psychiatry," rumbled Pnin, in his answer to Chateau. "Why not leave their private sorrows to people? Is sorrow not, one asks, the only thing in the world people really possess?" [51–52]

Always in Nabokov the most sensitive consciousnesses are those made to bear enormous pain. The essential equation between the maximum capability of suffering and the infliction of maximum suffering is Nabokov's predilection: the favorites get the worst treatment. Nabokov's interest is with the extraordinarily tender, imaginative, compassionate consciousness trying vainly to come to terms with time or death or human cruelty. Loss lends value.

And vulnerability at least implies loss and thus value. In the first chapter, Nabokov uses heart trouble to put Timofey Pnin on the brink. Pnin does not die, of course, but death provides the backdrop from this point on, and all the novel's activity takes on a highlight against the shadow of the eternal sleeping car. Even the wit turns toward the darkness that will claim us. The decorating and Pninizing of a brand-new office occasion an image even more surprising than that eternal sleeping car evoked by Nina's visit to Cook's in "Spring in Fialta": "With the help of the janitor [Pnin] screwed onto the side of the desk a pencil sharpener—that highly satisfying, highly philosophical implement that goes ticonderoga-ticonderoga, feeding on the yellow finish and sweet wood, and ends up in a kind of soundlessly spinning ethereal void as we all must" (69).

The novel achieves its most characteristic effect by infusing the ordinary, the domestic, the frail and charming commonplace with the rush of horror and tenderness that accompanies the remembrance of things that no longer exist. On the platform at Cremona, a little town where he is to lecture, Pnin is again transported by memory into the realm of ghosts, and a mad old aunt and his dead Mira both smile up at him. "Murdered, forgotten, unrevenged, incorrupt, immortal" (27), they will live as long as his consciousness lives.

Pnin the comic creation of the present is enlarged by Pnin the tragicomic remembrancer of the Russian past, as well as by Pnin with the bad heart, Pnin hopelessly in love, and most important of all, by Pnin the surrogate father—in a completely non-Freudian sense, of course—of Victor Wind. These references and points of contact radiating to and from Pnin keep him from being simply a very funny *object* (as he is to, say, Jack Cockerell, the chairman of the English Department and the best mimic of Pnin on campus); they make of Pnin the human and touching character that he is.

As we might expect, though, it is through the Nabokovian equivalent Victor that Pnin comes most painfully and lovably alive. Only a Nabokovian favorite can illuminate the highest possibilities of human consciousness.

Victor and Lake

Nabokov spares nothing in creating Victor as an equivalent; short of Van Veen in *Ada*, Victor Wind is perhaps Nabokov's most unflawed and precocious equivalent—at fourteen already the possessor of the taste, the political acumen, and the aloof superiority of such a genius as, say, Vladimir Nabokov. All of chapter 4 is devoted to him; and his gift to Pnin, a beautiful cut-glass punchbowl that Pnin uses at his "house-heating soirée," becomes the primary source of emotional energy for that important episode.

We are told, "Actually, Victor's father was a cranky refugee doctor [Eric Wind], whom the lad had never much liked and had not seen now for almost two years" (85). No bond between Victor and a grotesque like Eric Wind can be allowed by Nabokov, of course, so an exiled king in one of Victor's recurrent dreams is identified as his "more plausible father." The pressure of preserving the purity of the favorite's personality, genius, and good taste also necessitates a curious psychological maturity in a fourteen-year-old, and once more we find Nabokov casting mimicry aside for favoritism: Victor's attitude toward his mother, we are told, has altered so that "passionate childhood affection had long since been replaced by tender condescension" (87), and Victor acts with "amused submission" when she relates or invents exaggerated stories about him to strangers. What fourteen-year-old ever felt "amused submission" about anything? Where is the fourteen-year-old who does not hate, but *condescends?* Just as with the blurred presentation of Paduk, or with Kinbote, Nabokov mars his mimicry in the pursuit of his "own advantage," and characterization and plausibility are sacrificed.

Once again the Nabokovian favorite reduces the manipulators who surround him to cobwebs by insisting that they are preposterous, a process that reaches its apotheosis in *Invitation to a Beheading.* But Victor, like other Nabokovian favorites, poses a problem: the dramatic possibilities are very limited for such a brilliant, successful personality, and here there is no plausible source of melodrama to threaten him.

The passage presenting Lake, the resident painter at Victor's school, has little reference to the tale of Pnin, and defies organic integration into the narrative. It is an example of art-for-art's-sake and of that extremely important but impalpable characteristic of Nabokov's work which I can define no more closely than a "being-about-itself" rather than a "being-about-something." Lake is set into the novel for no other reason than to represent in it some of Nabokov's own theories and prejudices about art, and he of course appreciates and is appreciated by Victor. "While endowed with the morose temper of genius, [Lake] lacked originality and was aware of that lack. . . . Among the many exhilarating things Lake taught was that the order of the solar spectrum is not a closed circle but a spiral of tints from cadmium red and oranges through a strontian yellow and a pale paradisal green to cobalt blues and violets, at which point the sequence does not grade into red again but passes into another spiral, which starts with a kind of lavendar gray and goes on to Cinderella shades transcending human perception" (96).

The spiral again, Nabokov's "spiritualized circle" which avoids the viciousness of circles by becoming "etherealized." And this transcendence of finite physical terms and brute facts is surely one way toward the state of "aesthetic bliss" that is one function of art itself in Nabokov. Nowhere in Nabokov is there any accommodation on the part of his favorites to the brutal terms that time and death impose on us; and not only do the favorites furiously rattle the cage, but they *will* make an escape, even if it is only the private, subjective escape a Kinbote achieves.

Lake's spiral of tints is thus the spiral we find throughout Nabokov, the one that has no discernible destination but at least leads "in the right direction." Art is a kind of ecstasy, forever beyond time and death, where Platonic cave-shadows from another world assume the permanence of Altamira animals.

An evocation of the workshops of the Renaissance masters

combines the fantasies of both Victor and Lake into the over-voice, and there is a hint that Lake's artistic secondariness, like Kinbote's, may have some taint of sexual inversion: "[Victor] studied his mediums with the care and patience of an insatiable child—one of those painter's apprentices (it is now Lake who is dreaming!)', lads with bobbed hair and bright eyes who would spend years grinding colors in the workshop of some great Italian skiagrapher, in a world of amber and paradisal glazes" (98).

Nabokov's personality types are constants, no matter what the scale, and we enjoy our reading more if we are alert to the traits and codes which Nabokov habitually allies with them. We realize that a Nabokovian favorite loathes Freud, Marx, groups, and social climbers. But even the minor creations share the same few failings: failed art and inverted, or at least decadent, sexual pro-clivites are usually linked in Nabokov—almost as firmly as a philistine and his beloved progressive education and supermarket Muzak or, say, a second-rate mind with an abridged dictionary.

Unlike Shade's voice and consciousness in *Pale Fire,* Victor's consciousness adds nothing to *Pnin* that the overvoice can't supply as well or better, and since he is difficult to integrate into its action and meaning, he is abandoned after a short interlude when he visits Pnin, and survives only in his gift of the punch bowl. Victor-as-effect-on-Pnin is important, not Victor-as-con-sciousness. Risky as it may be constantly to judge a novel by what has been left out of it, I would venture to say that Victor is useful to Nabokov as a means of defining and enlarging Pnin, as a recipient of Pnin's emotion and attention rather than as a donor of consciousness to the novel as a whole; as a character—aloof, ironic, unscarred, friendly, brilliant, non-Oedipal, unambitious, successful, skeptical, wholly uninvolved, and with his artistic talent unrepresentable in the medium of words—he is something of a difficulty, if not a dead end. Only his subjective importance to Pnin remains and, triumphantly translated into the punch bowl, it brings the novel's most memorable and poignant effect.

Recurrence in *Pnin*

One mark of Pnin's nonequivalence to Nabokov, a distinction that separates Pnin's consciousness and sensibility wholly from those of the overvoice, is his reaction to the phenomena of recurrence and coincidence—those endlessly suggestive sources of speculation for a John Shade, a Fyodor, and a Humbert.

When Pnin takes lodgings at Laurence and Joan Clements' house, he lets a fascinating coincidence slip by because he does not have the turn of mind that would make much of it. Relating a long personal history to Joan ("a curriculum vitae in a nutshell— a coconut shell" [33]), Pnin notes that he had escaped to Constantinople in 1919 after the defeat of the White Army:

"Say, I was there as a child exactly the same year," said pleased Joan. "My father went to Turkey on a government mission and took us along. We might have met! I remember the word for water. And there was a rose garden . . ."

"Water in Turkish is 'su,' " said Pnin, a linguist by necessity, and went on with his fascinating past. [33]

Indifference to what Nabokov calls those phenomena which "cannot be stated, let alone solved" is part of Pnin's existence as object, part of the distance between him and the overvoice in which the story is told. It is quite obvious that the overvoice loves Pnin, but it is just as obvious that the overvoice and Pnin are quite distinct.

Pnin's house-warming party (or his "house-heating" as Pnin, a linguist by default, malaprops it) in the novel's next-to-last chapter is the occasion for gathering together many of the micro-motifs that have been visible at the edges of the novel's surface.

Throughout the narrative we have been getting little clues as to the existence of a mysterious literary man whose life has touched Pnin's—and Liza's. Gradually it becomes apparent that this man is also the narrator who occasionally (and arbitrarily) intrudes into the novel as a first-person voice, and who appears as both the narrator of the novel and a character in it in the last chapter, the consciousness I call "V.V."[3] Early in the novel we are told that Liza had "a rather silly affair with a littérateur who is now—but no matter." At the émigré hotel, Pnin and his friend Professor Chateau discuss the émigré writers "Bunin, Aldanov, Sirin" (117), and "Sirin" was, of course, Nabokov's *nom de plume*. A few pages later, Pnin and Chateau come upon some butterflies and wish that "Vladimir Vladimirovich" were there to tell them about the "enchanting insects" (128)—and Pnin lets at least one hot drop of rancor fall about this littérateur-scientist who had long ago captivated Liza, for he offers the opinion that V.V.'s entomological interests are "merely a pose."

V.V. is then a figure half in and half out of the novel's fictionality, for of course the real Nabokov is the entomological expert, and although a character might share his expertise, the joke would have no point unless it was being pulled by Nabokov on himself, and turned on what we know about *him*. When we learn that Pnin is going to be fired from Waindell, we are told that Pnin's courses will be taught by "a prominent Anglo-Russian writer," and this writer arrives on campus and replaces Pnin, on the latter's birthday, in the last chapter. It is again the "brilliant" and "fascinating" V.V. to whom Hagen refers when he breaks the news to Pnin about the firing at the bedraggled end of Pnin's housewarming. Earlier, while the party is still in full swing, the most subtle and important reference to this curious half-real, half-fictional V.V. has been carefully set into the dialogue; instead of being only another unit in a series of recurrent allusions, this reference is an important statement by Nabokov on his own art.

It is ten o'clock, "and Pnin's Punch and Betty's Scotch were causing some of the guests to talk louder than they thought they did" (159). Joan Clements enunciates the reference, punctuating it by "deep hawing pants": " 'But don't you think—haw—that what he is trying to do—haw—practically in all of his novels—haw—is—haw—to express the fantastic recurrence of certain situations?' " (159).

Thus in a muted, oblique manner, the art before us becomes, briefly, its own subject. Joan has been given an important Nabokovian artistic tenet to announce. In *Pnin* the micro-motifs once again signify the presence of a creative deity above and behind the work.

In the very first chapter we are told that Pnin had had a heart seizure on his birthday, February 15, 1937, the same day of the month that he leaves Waindell in the last chapter. The day in chapter 3 on which Pnin is presented to us first in the Waindell library, then as he goes to the campus Soviet films, and then finally losing his room at the Clements' to the return of the Clements' divorced daughter, is also his birthday. The presentation of this fact is oblique. "As usual he marched to the Periodicals Room and there glanced at the news in the latest (Saturday, February 12—and this was Tuesday, O Careless Reader!) issue of the Russian-language daily published, since 1918, by an émigré group in Chicago" (75).

Not only have we been told that it is Tuesday a few paragraphs before (and carelessly ignored it), but we have to have noted the date of Pnin's birthday to find out that this Tuesday is a special one, a birthday Tuesday. And if we go back a little further, we find Nabokov has been teasingly emphasizing the day and the date, but this micro-motif skims by, along with a great deal else:

[Pnin] did not possess (nor was he aware of this lack) any long *oo:* all he could muster when called upon to utter "noon" was the lax vowel of the German *"nun"* (I have no classes in after*nun* on Tuesday. Today is Tuesday.")

Tuesday—true; but what day of the month, we wonder. Pnin's birthday for instance fell on February 3, by the Julian calendar into which he had been born in St. Petersburg in 1898. He never celebrated it nowadays, partly because, after his departure from Russia, it sidled by in a Gregorian disguise (thirteen—no, twelve days late). [66–67]

Flaying the author of one recent study of his work, Nabokov gives us an important passage on the reading of Nabokov. Notice how everything that he says here turns our attitude back to the art as art, toward an attitude of art-about-itself, art up to its own proper business of expressing its own impulses and energies; art as an end rather than as a mediation, a translation, or a conveyance:

I wish to share [with this critic] the following secret: in the case of a certain type of writer it often happens that a whole paragraph or sinuous sentence exists as a discrete organism, with its own imagery, its own invocations, its own bloom, and then it is especially precious, and also vulnerable, so that if an outsider, immune to poetry and common sense, injects spurious symbols into it, or actually tampers with its wording . . . its magic is replaced by maggots. The various words [this critic] mistakes for the "symbols" of academic jargon, supposedly planted by an idiotically sly novelist to keep schoolmen busy, are not labels, not pointers, and certainly not the garbage cans of a Viennese tenement, but live fragments of specific description, rudiments of metaphor, and echoes of creative emotion.[4]

Thus the micro-motifs in Nabokov's work are a pattern of "intricate enchantment and deception" that mimics nature's most exhilarated and complex acts of "enchantment and deception." Nabokov does not fill his fiction with symbols; he marks it with the godly signatures of a proud and happy creator, a creator going about the business of creating art with the same vivacity that nature goes about its creation. Symbols lead us *out of* and *away from,* and seek to connect a work of art to a source of emotional or intellectual energy outside itself, whereas Nabokov's micro-motifs are usually self-contained, self referential, and lead us *back to, back within.* These micro-motifs are derived from the same cells and tissues of which the larger work is created. Even his allusions to the art of other artists are an allusion to art, nothing else, a creator indicating creation by pointing to the creations of colleague deities. Unlike Eliot, Nabokov is not using his art to state religious, cultural, or sociological convictions, nor do his allusions act as a shorthand or a code for cultural phenomena. *The Waste Land* is an economical lesson, and a profound one, in Western cultural history, and its allusions to Dante, Shakespeare, or the sexual etioliation of a twentieth-century typist form a prolonged and intricate statement about the quality of a dying Christian society; it is a work of persuasion; and it ultimately even offers a solution—a return to Christ. Thus its interests lie partially outside of art, and its art would, ideally, lead us through itself, beyond art, to things of which art is incapable. But Nabokov's art is terminal. It delights in itself. It teaches us nothing we can paraphrase. It does not persuade. And it leads back only to itself.

Coincidence and Villainy at the "House-Heating" Party

One of the micro-motifs that we follow right up through the party is Pnin's "Wynn-Twin" mixup, for he has invited the look-

alike instead of the ornithology professor he knows slightly, and
we watch Pnin dropping allusions and jokes about birds throughout the affair to a puzzled anthropologist, Professor Thomas. But,
coincidentally, it is Thomas who has set off the Pninian chain
reaction of mistaken identity by asking him about "a cake baked
in the form of a bird" in rural Russia—and Pnin, ignoring the
anthropologist's cant explanation of his interest ("Basically of
course, the symbol is phallic" [150]), but hearing his mention
of a bird, jumps with relief at this single misleading clue to which
of these look-alikes is which. So Thomas is mistakenly invited to
Pnin's house-warming. This mistake is more than a simple matter
of authorial amusement at Pnin's expense for, like the hideous
inkwell that Ferdinand in "Spring in Fialta" buys and discards,
it indicates a trajectory, and larger and more important things
will follow that trajectory.

Another of Pnin's guests is Betty Bliss, a former graduate
student of his whom he had at one time distantly qualified as a
plausible mate. "But . . . a diminutive diamond [ring] had
appeared on her plump hand, and this she displayed with coy
pride to Pnin, who vaguely experienced a twinge of sadness"
(152). Another opportunity lost forever. Although Pnin realizes
well enough that Betty has "a servant maid's mind" and that
nothing can "make her disbelieve in the wisdom and wit of her
favorite woman's magazine," the extinction of a possibility in
life is sad in itself. Here in *Pnin,* one more possibility is extinguished forever.

Nabokov is clearly preparing us for something when we learn
that "by some tender coincidence," a large aquamarine punch
bowl sent by Victor to Pnin from money he earned as a waiter
at Yosemite has arrived on the day of the party. Laurence
Clements finds, by coincidence, his exact likeness to "Jan van
Eyck's ample-jowled, fluff-haloed Canon van der Paele" (154)

in an album that, good things attaching only to good people, Victor has been given by his mother and has left with Pnin. By coincidence. Furthermore, a reader alert to Nabokov's habitual codes and alliances quickly sees the significance of the fact that Laurence is going to give the picture to his publisher to use as his own dust-jacket portrait: *trompe l'oeil*, the "subtle mimicry" of art by nature, is a satisfaction that only the very good minds of Nabokov's favorites perceive. Laurence's consciousness becomes important in this chapter, as we shall see; Nabokov is busy making him into a surrogate favorite as this party progresses and is conferring Nabokovian tints on him. Soon the bowl is again a subject of conversation; Pnin has no idea how much it cost— material valuation is irrelevant to Nabokov's beloved characters, of course—but Joan is awed enough by it to claim it must have cost Victor at least two hundred dollars, which impresses the reader, if not Pnin. And a curious metamorphosis starts to take place in Dr. Hagen, who has been introduced to us much earlier in the novel as a "pleasant, rectangular old man" and whom we last saw, while Pnin was offstage, futilely but faithfully defending Pnin's usefulness to Blorenge, the fraud and ass of a department chairman whose machinations make Timofey's dismissal necessary.

But now we learn that Hagen's daughter is twenty-four, and about to return from Europe, "where she had spent a wonderful summer touring Bavaria and Switzerland with a very gracious old lady, Dorianna Karen, famous movie star of the twenties" (158). No one voluntarily goes to or comes from Germany in Nabokov without being tainted by it. Hagen is a German, and there are no sympathetic Germans in any of Nabokov's novels or stories. The point is further developed in the conversation of the Clements when they are leaving the party: " 'I would never,' said Joan, as she backed the car and worked on the wheel, 'but *never*

have allowed my child to go abroad with that old Lesbian.'
'Careful,' said Laurence, 'he may be drunk but he is not out of
earshot' " (166)'.

The incidental fact that Joan, not Laurence, is driving the car
is in itself a minor but unambiguous clue to Nabokov's approval
of them and disapproval of Hagen; neither Shade nor Krug can
drive, nor can Nabokov. And we are told that Joan's husband is
his university's "most original and least liked scholar," a description that might also apply to Krug. It is generally true in Nabokov's work that, at the approach of harm—as in the confrontation between Krug and Paduk—either the overvoice is especially
busy and intrusive, fluttering about the favorite and reducing the
monster to only a magnified failure and neurotic of papier-
mâché (one function of Krug's sitting on Paduk's face in their
schooldays)', or that one character becomes more and more a
favorite, as Kinbote, for example, does at the approach of
Gradus. Here Nabokov has singled out Clements for this strange
investiture. Notice the contrast between the isolated Clements—
individual, nonconvivial—and the gossiping and salacious Hagen,
here passing on a good one:

In the bay end of the room, Clements kept morosely revolving the
slow globe as Hagen, carefully avoiding the traditional intonations
he would have used in more congenial surroundings, told him and
grinning Thomas the latest story about Mrs. Idelson, communicated
by Mrs. Blorenge to Mrs. Hagen. Pnin came up with a plate of
nougat.

"This is not quite for your chaste ears, Timofey," said Hagen to
Pnin, who always confessed he could never see the point of any
"scabrous anecdote." "However—"

Clements moved away to rejoin the ladies. Hagen began to retell
the story, and Thomas began to re-grin. Pnin waved a hand at the
raconteur in a Russian disgusted "oh-go-on-with-you" gesture and
said:

"I have heard quite the same anecdote thirty-five years ago in Odessa, and even then I could not undertsand what is comical in it." [159–160]

The code of values embodied in these micro-motifs is invariable: dirty stories, invasion of privacy, a German talking gleefully to an academic second-rater (who has himself been consigned to the darkness forever because he used the term "phallic"), perhaps the suggestion of genteel anti-Semitism in those "traditional intonations" and the name "Idelson." Contrast this with Clements and Pnin, who are bored, offended, quirky, slightly rude, and have none of the slickness or social "grace" that marks the successful operator. They both turn their backs on Hagen and Thomas, and keep themselves unsullied. Nabokov's divisions are scrupulous; further, he does not content himself with judging these people by means of the overvoice. Someone onstage must act out the role of favorite in order to disconcert or abuse the malign characters.

The Hagen metamorphosis is not yet completed, however, simply by gossip; when the subject of teaching is batted about later in the party, it is Hagen who takes a position that the student should be locked up in a sound-proof room with phonograph records and *without* a lecturer. While expounding this theory, Hagen is made to glance sharply and a little fearfully at Clements: Nabokov loved to lecture and was a spectacular success at it as a college professor, and Clements, Nabokov's equivalent at this point, holds up for ridicule Thomas's ideas: "Tom thinks the best method of teaching anything is to rely on discussion in class, which means letting twenty young blockheads and two cocky neurotics discuss for fifty minutes something that neither their teacher nor they know" (161). It remains for Pnin to deliver the most overt indictment of Hagen, for time is running out and Hagen has some bad news to give Timofey. "Hagen asked for a glass of water or beer. Whom does he remind me of? thought Pnin suddenly. Eric Wind? Why? They are quite different physically" (162).

The metamorphosis is now complete; Hagen is transformed into Eric Wind and so is at last suitably soiled to be the agent dealing the novel's sharpest blow of onstage evil, Pnin's dismissal. Why was it necessary for Nabokov to transform Hagen into Eric before this blow, especially since Hagen is not even responsible for it and is even trying to act kindly? Perhaps because Nabokov needs to have a set of very clear oppositions in his fiction, particularly at the worst moments, and to have characters embody these oppositions. There were indications that, as the suicide approached in "Triangle within Circle," Yasha was being gradually but steadily elevated, Rudolf degraded; here in *Pnin,* a novel in which, up to this point, evil has been only a European memory (Mira at Buchenwald), or only the remote logical extension of the stupidity of a generally comic character like Eric or Liza or Blorenge, at last we have a dramatic stroke of bad fortune, and in this situation Nabokov's feelings for his favorite character won't permit him to present the scene without having his representative right there to humiliate the destructive philistines. The Good and the good and the Evil and the evil are absolutely segregated once again. In Nabokov, they always are. And, quixotically enough, good people are always allowed a superior *gesture* that infuriates their evil counterparts; Krug has sat on Paduk's face; and Shade, although unable to humiliate his destroyer when he himself is really being destroyed, is allowed in his poem a prefabricated quixotic gesture of contempt for his assassin:

> But who can teach the thoughts we should roll-call
> When morning finds us marching to the wall
> Under the stage direction of some goon

Political, some uniformed baboon?
We'll think of matters only known to us—
Empires of rhyme, Indies of calculus;
Listen to distant cocks crow, and discern
Upon the rough gray wall a rare wall fern;
And while our royal hands are being tied,
Taunt our inferiors, cheerfully deride
The dedicated imbeciles and spit
Into their eyes just for the fun of it.

[Canto Three, 11.597–608]

But the subtle feelings of error and misfortune are not confined to Hagen's curious metamorphosis; several little signals occur just at the edge of the reader's perception. "Hagen could not find the cane he had come with (it had fallen behind a trunk in the closet)" (162). And Mrs. Thayer discovers she has left her purse, sends her husband back for it, and we discover that he has returned with the wrong bag. Just before learning of his dismissal, Pnin excitedly tells Joan Clements that on the morrow "under the curtain of mysteree, I will see a gentleman who is wanting to help me buy this house!" Hagen has a Bavarian grandfather, who gave him the walking stick, but one of its movable decorative parts is broken, as is his car. Professor Thomas wonders why Pnin called him "Professor Vin," that is, "Professor Wynn."

Thus, Hagen delivers his news of Pnin's dismissal to a reader who has been subtly alerted to error and misfortune and is now aware of Hagen himself as vaguely vile. Nothing that he says relieves this: "As my friend, Dr. Kraft [another German, of course] wrote me the other day: you, Herman Hagen, have done more for Germany in America than all our missions have done in Germany for America" (168).

Pnin's comment here to Hagen, and Hagen's vulgarized transformation of it, show how far apart they are:

"You and I will give next year some splendid new courses which I have planned long ago. On Tyranny. On the Boot. On Nicholas the First. On all the precursors of modern atrocity. Hagen, when we speak of injustice, we forget Armenian massacres, tortures which Tibet invented, colonists in Africa. . . . This history of man is the history of pain!"

Hagen bent over to his friend and patted him on his knobby knee.

"You are a wonderful romantic, Timofey, and under happier circumstances . . . however, I can tell you that in the Spring Term we *are* going to . . . stage a Dramatic Program. [168]

To receive Pnin's passionate discovery of history-as-pain as demonstrating him to be "a wonderful romantic" hints that Hagen is related to the Bachofen sisters. With a few more remarks—including the information about the "fascinating lecturer" under whom Pnin refuses to work—Hagen leaves, advising Pnin to put himself to sleep "with a good mystery story." It should come as no surprise to a careful analyst of Nabokov's personality codes to learn that Nabokov loathes mystery stories.

The chapter ends with Pnin washing all his dinnerware, including the precious punchbowl, and dropping a nutcracker into the suds with "an excruciating crack of broken glass":

Pnin hurled the towel into a corner and, turning away, stood for a moment staring at the blackness beyond the threshold of the open back door. A quiet, lacy-winged little green insect circled in the glare of a strong naked lamp above Pnin's glossy bald head. He looked very old, with his toothless mouth half open and a film of tears dimming his blank, unblinking eyes. Then, with a moan of anguished anticipation, he went back to the sink and, bracing himself, dipped his hand into the foam. A jagger of glass stung him. Gently he removed a broken goblet. The beautiful bowl was intact. He took a fresh dish towel and went on with his household work.
[172–173]

The power of this passage depends on Pnin's not having the resources of a Nabokovian authorial favorite, on his being set all alone, as object, against "the blackness beyond the threshold of the open back door"; the smallness, ordinariness, and vulnerability of Pnin's life and career make the bowl much more than a metaphor for that fragility. It is one of the very few magical objects in a very meager life. Unlike Krug, Pnin has no one above him to take care of him; and a broken punchbowl, in the context of *Bend Sinister,* would have little emotional power measured as it would have to be against the monstrousness of the Padukian state. Here in Pnin's life, the bowl is more than enough—so much more than enough that it is hard to believe that Nabokov can carry through the ethical tenet he enunciates as Pnin finally finds a way to Cremona in the first chapter: "Some people—and I am one of them—hate happy ends. We feel cheated. Harm is the norm. Doom should not jam. The avalanche stopping in its tracks a few feet above the cowering village behaves not only unnaturally but unethically" (25).

Pnin is always skating over an abyss of brute fact: Mira, his parents, his bad heart, the precariousness of his career, his hopeless love for Liza, none of which he can really deal with at all; they must be avoided. If we cannot "jam doom" we must look the other way. Pnin must continually protect himself from the brutal facts of finitude. Avoidance of endings naturally characterizes his scholarship. "[His] research had long entered the charmed stage when the quest overrides the goal, and a new organism is formed, the parasite so to speak of the ripening fruit. Pnin averted his mental gaze from the end of his work, which was so clearly in sight that one could make out the rocket of an asterisk, the flare of a 'sic!' This line of land was to be shunned as the doom of everything that determined the rapture of endless approximation" (143).

"Endless approximation" is thus Pnin's mode of consciousness. There is, just behind his "averted" mental gaze, only the empty and hopeless vulnerability to the brute fact that a fantast like Kinbote prefers to leave far behind. But Pnin must sustain himself or fail on the basis of fact; he has no large and systematic illusion with which to defend himself. Therefore a life of process rather than ends is his solution, "endless approximation" rather than brute facts. The facts can *never* be faced by any of Nabokov's favorites. Perhaps that is why Nabokov preserves the bowl: he has nothing else to offer Pnin.

5

Lolita

The Problem of Favoritism

Lolita is Nabokov's most complex novel in terms of its moral scheme. It is also his most triumphant integration of character and plot or, more precisely, of voice and activity.

In looking at the novel's moral scheme, one should attend particularly to what is missing from it. Humbert, Charlotte, and Lolita form their own triangle in a circle, and to be able to enjoy Lolita without interference, Humbert need only murder Charlotte. He recognizes this fact and even toys with the idea in his diary, and Nabokov presents him the perfect opportunity for murder when Charlotte and Humbert go swimming at Hourglass Lake while Lolita is away at camp. But Humbert cannot go through with it, and his failure is due not to the lack of any "simple energy," but to his moral repugnance:

The setting was really perfect for a brisk bubbling murder, and here was the subtle point. The [retired policeman and retired plumber building a dock] were just near enough to witness an accident and just far enough not to observe a crime. . . . I knew that all I had to do was to drop back, take a deep breath, then grab her by the ankle and rapidly dive with my captive corpse. . . . And when some twenty minutes later the two puppets steadily growing arrived in a rowboat, one half newly painted, poor Mrs. Humbert . . . the victim of a cramp or coronary occlusion, or both, would be standing on her head in the inky ooze, some thirty feet below the smiling surface of Hourglass Lake.

Simple, was it not? But what d'ye know, folks—I just could not make myself do it. [88–89]

Humbert's inability to kill Charlotte is one example of Nabokov's playing favorites, for the author has preserved Humbert's appeal by distinguishing his lust from murderousness. By stopping Humbert short at that point, Nabokov proves to us that even in the perfect situation for murder, Humbert cannot kill. His refusal is a moral achievement. If Charlotte is to die, her death must be the result of extrahuman agencies; and it is indeed fate that Humbert perceives as the cause of the automobile accident which makes his adventures with Lolita possible:

I had actually seen the agent of fate [Frederick Beale, Jr., who drove the "death vehicle"]. . . . A brilliant and monstrous mutation had taken place, and here was the instrument. Within the intricacies of the pattern (hurrying housewife, slippery pavement, a pest of a dog, steep grade, big car, baboon at its wheel), I could dimly distinguish my own vile contribution. Had I not been such a fool—or such an intuitive genius—to preserve that journal, fluids produced by vindictive anger and hot shame would not have blinded Charlotte in her dash to the mailbox. But even had they blinded her, still nothing might have happened, had not precise fate, that synchronizing phantom, mixed with its alembic the car and the dog and the sun and the shade and the wet and the weak and the strong and the stone. Adieu, [Charlotte]! Fat fate's formal handshake (as reproduced by Beale before leaving the room) brought me out of my torpor; and I wept. Ladies and gentlemen of the jury—I wept. [105]

By making "precise fate" responsible for the tragedy, Nabokov maintains Humbert's humanity if not his unequivocal innocence;

and although we are going to hear a great deal about "McFate" throughout the novel, Charlotte's death is the only important incident in the novel that occurs outside the normal boundaries of cause and effect, or of human personality expressing itself in human activity. It is by far the most important intervention in the book from outside the frame of its fictional reality. The purpose of this unlikely and singular intervention seems to be the desire on Nabokov's part to keep Humbert's appeal intact, and nothing else.

But not only is Humbert kept from cold-blooded murder; Nabokov saves him from the act of actually deflowering precocious Dolores Haze. Charlie Holmes, the "coarse and surly but indefatigable" son of the headmistress of the aptly named Camp Climax, has spent "every blessed morning" of Lo's stay there copulating by turns with her and her friend Barbara in the "beautiful innocent forest brimming with all the emblems of youth." By showing that Lolita's sexual corruption predated Humbert's contribution to it, Nabokov once again shifts moral responsibility away from his favorite. Humbert's crime is kept within strict limits: he is no killer of innocent women and no deflowerer of innocent children. Fate creates the parental vacuum into which his love and lust proceed. Even then it turns out to be Lo's own sexual corruption that initiates their relationship: "I am going to tell you something strange: it was she who seduced me. . . . Suffice it to say that not a trace of modesty did I perceive in this beautiful hardly formed young girl whom modern co-education, juvenile mores, the campfire racket and so forth had utterly and hopelessly depraved" (134–135).

In moral terms, then, Humbert is not wholly responsible for his own entry into his relationship with Lolita: fate kills Charlotte, and Lolita seduces him. That Humbert's impurity contributes the lesser share to the crime is evidence to me of Nabokov's willingness to preserve the moral integrity of his favorites at the expense of almost all other factors in his work. This willingness may well be looked at as a rigid and basic given of his fiction, a prejudice that limits the plot activity in his novels.

Humbert's real crime is keeping Lolita in captivity by means of bullying and blackmail—granting that the reader, if not the legal system, puts aside as only a technicality the question of statutory rape. And here we of course condemn him. But even this unpleasant bond of coercive intimidation—and it is emphasized several times by a cackling Humbert ("I succeeded in terrorizing Lo")—is qualified by several factors that relieve Humbert of pure monstrousness and make of him something a great deal more human and sympathetic than a cardboard Svengali. For one thing, he is rendered foolish and not a little pathetic in his attempts to keep Lolita "happy." The essential comic leverage of the novel is provided by the slide into teen-neon-roadside America of that extraordinarily sophisticated, refined and cosmopolitan intelligence, the involvement of that sensibility in Lolita's enchanting beauty and "eerie vulgarity"—and in America's. Whereas the novel's comedy depends on Humbert's ensnaring himself in the meretricious foolishness of Lolita and mid-century America, the novel's pathos, or tragedy, depends on Humbert's awareness of the authentic beauty of his mistress and of America, and on the contrast between the possibilities of his consciousness and the Procrustean violence to which Lolita and America subject that consciousness: "A great user of roadside facilities, my unfastidious Lo would be charmed by toilet signs—Guys-Gals, John-Jane, Jack-Jill, and even Buck's-Doe's; while lost in an artist's dream, I would stare at the honest brightness of the gasoline paraphernalia against the splendid gleam of oaks, or at a distant hill scrambling out—scarred but still untamed—from the wilderness of agriculture that was trying to swallow it" (155).

Although no easy equation between Humbert's two great discoveries, Lolita and America, ought to be enforced, they are obviously composed of the same cells and tissues. Humbert, composed of other stuff, necessarily offers a perspective that is
outside both of them: "On especially tropical afternoons, in the
sticky closeness of the siesta, I liked the cool feel of armchair
leather against my massive nakedness as I held her in my lap.
There she would be, a typical kid picking her nose while engrossed in the lighter sections of a newspaper, as indifferent to my
ecstasy as if it were something she had sat upon, a shoe, a doll,
the handle of a tennis racket, and was too indolent to remove"
(167).

In this manner, Humbert's narration and perspective offer us
his passion and yet an ironic qualification and placement of that
passion, "a shoe, a doll, the handle of a tennis racket," that make
it more than a little ludicrous. And yet it is only through his sensibility that the beauty in Lolita and America are made available
to us, for both the young girl and the New World are partially
unconscious of themselves: "Not only had Lo no eye for scenery
but she furiously resented my calling her attention to this or that
enchanting detail of landscape; which I myself learned to discern
only after being exposed for quite a time to the delicate beauty
ever present in the margin of our undeserving journey" (154).

Thus, many different factors work to keep Humbert out of the
center of our conception of moral crime and our condemnation
of it, to maintain his status as a Nabokovian favorite: he does not
kill Charlotte; he does not seduce Lolita; his sexual enjoyment
of her is imperfect because of her indifference; her thralldom to
him depends in part on her own indifference, rootlessness, and
meretriciousness, for Lolita wants to be entertained. Humbert
goes to enormous lengths to try to make her happy, and she en-
courages this. He is in the grip of a very real passion, is constantly

aware of his own guilt, and does not fool himself about the cruelty for which he *is* responsible: "I catch myself thinking today that our long journey had only defiled with a sinuous trail of slime the lovely, trustful, dreamy, enormous country that by then, in retrospect, was no more to us than a collection of dogeared maps, ruined tour books, old tires, and her sobs in the night —every night, every night—the moment I feigned sleep" (177– 178).

There are perhaps three additional factors that have a subtle effect on our moral sense. In the first place, only Humbert, within the novel, can create for us the images of beauty and tenderness that give the whole experience its "durable pigments." As we shall see, Quilty, in all other respects so similar to Humbert, is wholly incapable of this genius. Second, even as he is writing his *Confession,* Humbert has indeed *lost* his Lolita. And last, he is in jail when he writes the book and dead when we read it; and just as in the case of Nina's "lies" and "gibberish" in the story "Spring in Fialta," the death that puts an end to everything forms such a midnight background to human folly that our moral sense is reduced to relative triviality in comparison to the eternal sleeping car.

All of these factors modify our judgment of his crime, especially the ultimate failure of his falling in love with Mrs. Richard Schiller, and discovering that she simply does not care. Neither his love nor his crime, then, makes much of a difference to anyone but himself, and his self-imposed suffering seems to be his own most appropriate punishment.

Martin Green's brilliant analysis of *Lolita* pays a great deal of attention to the moral placement of the narrator. Green points out that the very intensity of Humbert's passion becomes a moral factor in the reader's mind: "The sexually perverse enterprises of the main character are made funny, beautiful, pathetic, ro-

mantic, tragic; in five or six different ways we are made to sympathize with him in them. Above all, they are made impressive.
. . . Wanting [so much] is an achievement not to be taken for granted. Humbert . . . does want Lolita fully; he does love her.
. . . The novel thus breaks down one of our most important and powerful taboos."[1]

The point of my argument thus far is to establish that Humbert is a favorite, and Nabokov, in protecting his favorites from our condemnation or dislike, is hardly the icy puppeteer both he and his critics keep giving to us as the Nabokov persona. If the novel included no Quilty, Humbert would still be less than fully criminal in our minds. He is, after all, the most attractive character in it. But Nabokov aims to give his narrator complete moral purgation—as well as to introduce a dramatic conflict into the narrative—and Quilty is his instrument in fulfilling these aims, moral and dramatic. We shall take a closer look at this creation to see if the moral atmosphere of *Lolita* corresponds to anything we have met in Nabokov before.

Clare Quilty, Clearly Guilty

Martin Green finds Quilty so useful to Humbert that he even speculates that Quilty may have been Humbert's invention, a private and subjective creation, like Kinbote's Gradus: "The similarity of their mental habits and sexual tastes, the differentiation between their moral guilts, the hallucinatory atmosphere of their encounter, the cousinly and indeed brotherly relationship foisted upon them—by all these hints we are invited to believe that Humbert Humbert first invented Quilty, to take on the worst of his own guilt, and then kills him, to purge himself symbolically."[2]

It would be difficult to make a good case for Humbert's fantasizing of a *Doppelgänger* from the novel itself. Although Humbert has been in mental institutions several times, and although the "cryptogrammic paper chase" between Quilty and Humbert which takes place after Quilty has wooed away Lolita frequently verges on a fantasy private to Humbert, we do not have a closed system of fantasy as we did with Kinbote's tale. A Foreword written by the redoubtable "John Ray, Jr.," precedes the *Confession of a White Widowed Male,* and the addition to this mimicked voice and point of view suggests that Humbert's tale is not merely a madman's invention—as Zembla was Kinbote's. I see little other purpose for the recapitulation and authentication of the novel's facts here, "outside" of the pages of the story itself.

Although Quilty evidently exists on the same plane of fictional reality that Humbert and Lolita occupy, his sexual interest in Lolita and his personality are quite carefully constructed—by Nabokov, not Humbert—to make his destruction a moral purgation for Humbert, the favorite. We even find that Nabokov once again uses his racial codes to stigmatize Quilty as inky villain. In the hilarious confrontation just before Humbert kills him, Quilty indicts himself in the following manner: " 'I am willing to try,' he said. 'You are either Australian, or a German refugee. Must you talk to me? This is a Gentile's house, you know. Maybe, you'd better run along. And do stop demonstrating that gun. I've an old Stern-Luger in the music room' " (299).

This is the same process that Hagen underwent in his stigmatization, although here the inks are darker.

Alfred Appel, Jr., points out the micro-motif of anti-Semitism that runs through *Lolita* and notes that Humbert is at least three times mistaken for a Jew. Quilty's pistol is a German one. And he tells Humbert he has been called "the American Maeterlinck." Then, quite rapidly, we learn that Quilty is not only a pornophile and an anti-Semite, but that he is also impotent and that his perversion extends all the way to executions: "Moreover I can arrange for you to attend executions, not everybody knows that the chair is painted yellow" (304).

Although Humbert finds Quilty all alone in his monstrous Pavor Manor, the playwright's destruction takes place just as a group of sinister guests arrive to accompany him to some unidentified "game." It is not misguided to think of these groups as standing for Nabokov's vision of society, or at least proving by their existence, even their success, the extent to which the social organism, in contrast to the individual conscience, is incapable of resisting putrefaction.

I stopped in the doorway and said: "I have just killed Clare Quilty." "Good for you," said the florid fellow as he offered one of the drinks to the elder girl. "Somebody ought to have done it long ago," remarked the fat man. "What does he say, Tony?" asked a faded blonde from the bar. "He says," answered the florid fellow, "he has killed Cue." "Well," said another unidentified man rising in a corner where he had been crouchng to inspect some records, "I guess we all should do it to him some day." [306–307]

The reaction of these people to Quilty's death is evil rather than ironic; the "good for you" and the "I guess we all should do it to him one day" are in some measure a just evaluation of Quilty's life and its worthlessness; Nabokov helps out Humbert's moral cause with this testimony from Quilty's playfellows. Their indifference to Quilty's criminality, although they are perfectly capable of perceiving his crime, is entirely representative of everything that is *not* Humbert in this novel.

As for the murder of Quilty itself, it is revenge on Humbert's part, but it is also of course much more than that. Quilty fails to perceive Lolita as anything but an object, and Humbert's perception of Lolita's humanity is what makes his murder of Quilty so purgative—for in this sense Quilty represents Humbert's old opportunism, his old selfishness, and his crime. It is important in understanding the novel's moral scheme to notice that Humbert comes to kill Quilty fresh from losing utterly and forever his Mrs. Richard Schiller, pregnant and impoverished, in Coalmont. That interview with Lolita is the novel's moral crucible in the sense that the elements that go into it come out transformed, and the transformation allows Humbert to see a last through his "sterile and selfish vice" into his real love:

I knew all I wanted to know. I had no intention of torturing my darling. Somewhere beyond Bill's shack an afterwork radio had begun singing of folly and fates, and there she was with her ruined looks and her adult, rope-veined narrow hands and her gooseflesh white arms, and her shallow ears, and her unkempt armpits, there she was (my Lolita!), hopelessly worn at seventeen, with that baby, dreaming already in her of becoming a big shot and retiring around 2020 A.D.—and I looked and looked at her, and knew as clearly as I know I am to die, that I loved her more than anything I had ever seen or imagined on earth, or hoped for anywhere else. [279]

Quilty's total incapacity for the love and redemption and self-knowledge and passion that Humbert is capable of provides an absolute distinction between the two men and gives a sense of justice to Humbert's execution of Quilty.

Not only is Quilty an unredeemable monster, but the society violated by Humbert's murder of him is also corrupt. It is no accident that Quilty is rich and successful, that he has "friends" on the police force, access to executions, a whole group of fellow-degenerates with whom to play, a reputation as an outstanding playwright. One small demonstration of the septic social norms within the novel is that Quilty's play *The Enchanted Hunters* has been chosen by the Beardsley thespians to perform. The world that surrounds Humbert, forbidding his sexual contact with

Lolita and his killing of Quilty, is corrupt—far more corrupt, at the core, than Humbert himself.

Gaston Godin, the lovable eccentric of Beardsley town, is presented to us for no other purpose than to alert us to the nether side of the Norman Rockwell sentimental archetype:

> I am loath to dwell so long on the poor fellow (sadly enough, a year later, during a voyage to Europe, from which he did not return, he got involved in a *sale histoire,* in Naples of all places!). I would have hardly alluded to him at all had not his Beardsley existence had such a queer bearing on my case. I need him for my defense. There he was, devoid of any talent whatsoever, a mediocre teacher, a worthless scholar, a glum repulsive fat old invert, highly contemptuous of the American way of life, triumphantly ignorant of the English language—there he was in priggish New England, crooned over by the old and caressed by the young—oh, having a grand time and fooling everybody; and here was I. [185]

The sentimental gauze which surrounds and disguises Gaston is part of the relentless self-deception that all philistines practice in this novel. Quilty and his play and career and friends are corrupt; so, of course, is Gaston; and so is cruel, hyper-middle-class Charlotte; and John Farlow, solid burgher and anti-Semite; and Mona Dahl, Lo's classmate, who has already had an affair with a marine; and Mary Lore, the nurse in Elphinstone, who helps Lo escape with Quilty; and, of course, Pratt, the head-mistress of Beardsley School, whose speeches are the longest and most socially significant in the novel. As she tells Humbert when he enrolls Lolita:

> "That is, with due respect to Shakespeare and others, we want our girls to *communicate* freely with the live world around them rather than plunge into musty old books. We are still groping perhaps, but we grope intelligently, like a gynecologist feeling a tumor.

. . . Dr. Hummer, do you realize that for the modern pre-adolescent child, medieval dates are of less vital value than weekend ones [twinkle]?—to repeat a pun that I heard the Beardsley college psychoanalyst permit herself the other day. We live not only in a world of thoughts, but also in a world of things. Words without experience are meaningless. What on earth can Dorothy Hummerson care for Greece and the Orient with their harems and slaves?"

[179–180]

Even politely ignoring Nabokov's opportunism in elbowing past mimetic fidelity in order to get in a good one ("like a gynecologist feeling a tumor"), we find that the philistine attitudes expressed by Pratt in her two long scenes square well enough with Nabokov's distaste for progressive education, generalities, vague "communication," and psychoanalysts to stand for almost everything in the novel outside Humbert's sensibility. For Nabokov's purposes, Pratt *is* society; she *is* genteel America. The entire world of normative values the novel offers us outside Humbert's own sensibility is more or less composed of Gastons, Charlottes, Pratts, Quiltys, and nothing else, certainly nothing positive. This is not to say that Humbert is absolved of his crime merely because his sensibility is clearly superior to everything about it. But his moral achievement, which forms the novel's final vision, his ultimate recognition of Lolita's humanity and his ultimate recognition of the violence and evil for which he is responsible by the theft of Lolita's childhood, has little to do with the mores and morals of mid-century America. Humbert tells us he quotes an "old poet" when he gives us the following gnomic couplet:

The moral sense in mortals is the duty
We have to pay on mortal sense of beauty. [285]

There is no "old poet," the couplet is Nabokov's own; more important, it is a characteristically extrasocial formulation. The esthetic consciousness, he states, does not exist in isolation from the moral consciousness: they are inseparably fused; there *are* inadmissible crimes; our acts do count—not in terms of society, for society is hopelessly corrupt—but they do count in the "infinite run" of things. The universe does make moral sense and demand moral discrimination. Even if life is a joke, human nature is incapable of surrendering to it, and the moral sense continues to smart and burn against even existential logic. If a "sense of sin" is not a supreme fact, it is a human one that no logic can assuage.

The gnomic couplet caps one of Humbert's most significant asides, and places his crime in a moral context much larger than any a social backdrop could provide. "Unless it can be proven to me—to me as I am now, today, with my heart and my beard, and my putrefaction—that in the infinite run it does not matter a jot that a North American girl-child named Dolores Haze had been deprived of her childhood by a maniac, unless this can be proven (and if it can, then life is a joke), I see nothing for the treatment of my misery but the melancholy and very local palliative of articulate art" (285).

Humbert's murder of Quilty is spurred on, then, at least in part, by moral imperatives. And his motives, in contrast to all else within the novel, spring from a moral epiphany that no one else in the novel could appreciate or even apprehend, let alone act upon. Morality in Nabokov always refers to a set of extrasocial truths, almost to a set of Platonic "universals" that are out of the reach of the philistine he dismisses as a "hairless ape" in the short story "Lance."

In the passage just quoted we have the first reference to the elements of this *Confession of a White Widowed Male* being alchemized into "articulate art." Here art is only a "palliative" for Humbert's stinging conscience, furnishing a relief but not a cure. Yet in the book's final passage, art, those "durable pigments," although still not a cure or a justification, is at least a significant gesture, a tribute if not a transformation; and only Humbert can offer that significant tribute, "the only immortality you and I may share," art itself, the "durable pigments."

A similar coda might have been spoken by his immortalizer to Krug, for it is only in art that Nabokov and Krug can share "immortality." But since the created never lived and the creator cannot live forever, this "immortality" is unfortunately only what Nabokov described it to be in *Bend Sinister:* "a play upon words." As always, in "the infinite run," time and death triumph, and only art, not the creator of art, survives. This paradox furnishes a pivotal meaning in *Bend Sinister,* in the story "Spring in Fialta" in the mortal difference between Nina and Ferdinand, and here in *Lolita;* John Shade's poem and his life form a complex statement about it, and *Ada* also employs it. It is one of Nabokov's most significant and suggestive themes.

Humbert, Lolita, and America

All of Nabokov's later fiction gives us a vision of two worlds, and of two or more kinds of consciousness. In *Bend Sinister,* Krug and the reader gradually perceive that the verisimilar narrative plane of fictional reality is being penetrated by its creator; and the second world, the world of the creator, completely eclipses that of the narrative in the novel's last passage. Even the verisimilar novel *Pnin* offers a sense of doubleness, of a world behind the world, not through any violation of its verisimilar plane, but in terms of the immediacy of the past, which is, paradoxically, completely dead—Russia and those Pnin loved have all been destroyed—and yet, they are fully alive in his consciousness, even quite capable of crowding into the foreground of it. A curious sense of a menacing, penetrating fate lurks just behind the scrim of reality in "Spring in Fialta," and one of the story's subtlest effects plays upon the difference between life and art, two absolutely distinct worlds. *Pale Fire* depends for its irony on the reader's perception of Kinbote's fantasy. Vasili in "Cloud, Castle, Lake" thought he could live in his fantasy, in his second world. The mad young fantasts of the stories "Lance" and "Signs and Symbols" and Luzhin in *The Defense* create complicated second worlds—wholly subjective, yet both terrible and wonderful in the completeness and energy with which they are endowed.

The sense of two worlds is important to *Lolita*, too—the world of facts, sunshine, respectability, common sense, white New England steeples, retired plumbers, polite anti-Semitism, local brides holding bouquets and wearing glasses, the world of time and death. And then there is, behind and beyond this, a world of heart's desire, a world of sensuality, timelessness, deathlessness, love. This world, like that perceivable to us through "aesthetic bliss," is a state of being wherein "curiosity, tenderness, kindness, ecstasy" are constant rather than intermittent.

For a good while Humbert performs a feat that usually eludes the Nabokovian fantast: he manages to live out his fantasy in the objective world. Humbert's sexual obsessions with girl-children are not purely sensual, and the unconsummated love affair he and his Annabel suffered on a Riviera beach is not for him simply a matter that can be redressed by availing himself of Lolita's fair young flesh. His recourse to young girls is a metaphysical as well as a physical complusion. It is a means of regaining something ineffably surrendered to time and fact. He is, like all of Nabokov's equivalents, a fantast by preference rather than to a factualist, for the cardinal quality of a fact is that nothing can be done with it. The supreme Nabokovian facts—time and death —are simply not to be faced, and Humbert's pedophilia, like Pnin's scholarship, is a process, a means rather than an end, an exit from time, an escape from fact: "It may well be that the

very attraction immaturity has for me lies not so much in the
limpidity of pure young forbidden fairy child beauty as in the
security of a situation where infinite perfections fill the gap between the little given and the great promised—the great rosegray
never-to-be-had" (266). Humbert is engaged in a form of art—
mimicry—that is much more immediate and fascinating than the
arbitrary and discarnate philosophy or creation in which the
usual Nabokovian favorite is engaged. Krug, for example, is a
"great philosopher"; he thinks and he writes, and we do indeed
get a few samples of his thought and writing. But there is no
direct means by which thinking and writing can operate as
dramatic or narrative activity. Once we follow Krug's thinking
or writing, we have abandoned the dramatic or narrative mode
and allowed Nabokov to substitute for this plane of activity one
of art-as-subject, of comment and of speculation. This phenomenon is even more striking when we are presented with Fyodor's
entire book on Chernyshevski, which forms chapter 4 of *The
Gift;* and Van Veen's *Texture of Time,* which is equally as inorganic dramatically.

Humbert's situation is also that of an artist. But his subject is
the integration of *himself* into his chosen problem, his given
milieu: like that of a voyeur, a spy,[3] a hunter, an anthropologist
among cannibals, Humbert's task is to slip unnoticed through the
habitat of his quarry in order to carry out his own ulterior purposes, and his art is that of successful mimicry, the blending of his
"stripes" upon the patterned "surface" of mid-century America, its
motels, its genteel pretensions, its masked neuroses, its subteen sub-
world. Here, we have the "mimetic subtlety, exuberance, and
luxury" which Nabokov admires so much in nature's most protean
insect mimes; and, best of all, the plot activity can express them. In
Lolita, the monster's whole business is to insinuate himself, for
sensual purposes, into the real world of mid-century America.

This insinuation offers dramatic and narrative possibilities that even Kinbote's situation fails to provide.

Kinbote, too, is engaged in a desperate game of mimicry and deception, but his fantasy, his lost Zembla, bears little resemblance to any actual place, least of all to mid-century America. In *Lolita,* the very sounds, scenes, and details of the fantasy-milieu, mid-century America, generate in Americans the deepest sort of interest in themselves, for here the terms of our society and life style are brilliantly observed and recorded. Martin Green points out quite rightly that "we are amused, amazed, deeply moved, merely by recognizing the language we hear around us every day." He affirms the brilliant success of Nabokov and Salinger in creating styles that do justice to America, but when he calls Humbert's voice a vehicle for "rococo realism," I believe he misses the pivot of Nabokov's success in *Lolita:* "This realism, despite its criticalness, its exasperation, its recurrent disgust, despite the inner convolutions and destructiveness . . . is a kind of affirmation of the American scene and of the possibility of life in America. But it is a rococo affirmation, playful, ornamental, lyrical, precarious; the style is a kind of American rococo."[4]

I think that the exhilaration that Martin Green took to be an affirmation of life in America is present only in Humbert's quite specialized, quite monstrous voice; it is not present in Kinbote's or Shade's; and those possibilities, that exuberance, do not really seem to illuminate Pnin's life.

It is not America itself or any realism, rococo or otherwise, that exhilarates Humbert and allows Nabokov to create Humbert's "playful, ornamental, lyrical" voice. The exhilaration seems to me to spring from the perfect integration of Humbert's character with his problem, Humbert's voice with a plot that makes his sexuality, his pursuit of "the great rosegray never-to-be-had," his comic-pathetic entanglement with the brainless beauty of

Lolita and the New World so beautiful and funny and touching all at once.

Does the novel really affirm the possibilities of American life? In the novel's climactic scene, Humbert finally falls in love with Mrs. Richard Schiller. But Lolita, meretricious and far less vulnerable then Humbert, dismisses Humbert's metamorphosis as irrelevant, almost silly: "She considered me as if grasping all at once the incredible—and somehow tedious, confusing and unnecessary—fact that the distant, elegant, slender, forty-year-old valetudinarian in velvet coat sitting beside her had known and adored every pore and follicle of her pubescent body. In her washed-out gray eyes, strangely spectacled, our poor romance was for a moment reflected, pondered upon, and dismissed like a dull party, like a rainy picnic to which only the dullest bores had come, like a humdrum exercise, like a bit of dry mud caking her childhood" (274).

Once more, the brainless and lobotomized triumph through sheer indifference.[5] And once more, the sensibilities of greatest subtlety, sensitivity, and vulnerability are singled out for the cruelest blows. This passage indicates no real possibilities of life in the American mode; quite the opposite. The Schillers *are* America, just as Charlotte is. Life for the consciousness of real sensitivity is impossible in the terms the novel presents to us: to this Lolita, to this Mrs. Richard Schiller, Humbert is simply "a bit of dry mud caking her childhood," and her ultimate triumph —a triumph she is incapable of even appreciating—is her indifference to him, her preference for Quilty over him, her choice— the proper one for her—of a Mrs. Richard Schillerdom over anything he could offer. She and her Dick are going to go to Alaska and make big money; she has no use for Humbert. This extinguishes him utterly. All that he can do is to remove Quilty, a *real* monster, from the world, an act of which we of course fully approve but Lolita would not. Quilty is not a monster to her, nor is he to the society which tolerates and even rewards him.

After the murder, when Humbert is at last standing beside the enormous valley while he waits for the police to fetch him, his final vision of his crime is of a moral sensitivity completely beyond Lolita's capabilities: "What I heard was but the melody of children at play, nothing but that. . . . I knew that the hopelessly poignant thing was not Lolita's absence from my side, but the absence of her voice from that concord" (309–310).

The poignancy of this loss afflicts only Humbert. Mrs. Richard Schiller, who finds Quilty a "genius," who finds Humbert only some "dry mud caking her childhood," and who is busy incubating a philistine fetus in her stretched belly, is not given this sensitivity.

The crime for which Humbert is responsible is a crime against his own ethical sense rather than against Lolita, for she is quite as indifferent to the injury he supposes he has done her as she is indifferent to his love of her. In this instance, "crime" is a wholly subjective affair, existing only in the mind of the criminal.

Notice the light-years of difference between Lolita's consciousness and Humbert's as he leaves her for the last time:

"One last word," I said in my horrible careful English, "are you quite, quite sure that—well, not tomorrow, of course, and not [the day] after tomorrow, but—well—some day, any day, you will not come to live with me? I will create a brand new God and thank him with piercing cries, if you give me that microscopic hope" (to that effect).

"No," she said smiling, "no."

"It would have made all the difference," said Humbert Humbert.

Then I pulled out my automatic—I mean, this is the kind of a fool thing a reader might suppose I did. It never even occurred to me to do it.

"Good by-aye!" she chanted, my American sweet immortal dead love; for she is dead and immortal if you are reading this. I mean, such is the formal agreement with the so-called authorities. [282]

Thus, neither Lolita nor America is presented to Humbert as a real possibility. Quite the opposite: life is utterly impossible for Humbert on their terms. The exhilaration in Humbert's tone is not any simple exhilaration with the mid-century American scene. In fact, in his Afterword notes "On a Book Entitled *Lolita,*" Nabokov indicates a certain gleeful reveling in Lolita's and America's lobotomized but lively vulgarity: "Nothing is more exhilarating than philistine vulgarity" (317).

But Humbert's delight in the "philistine vulgarity" seems to be more complex than any simple Camp experience, any simple superiority; the stripes and patterns of that surface are, after all, the terms of his own elaborate "deception" and "mimicry." The American milieu is not simply savaged for comic effect; it contains an irreplaceable, irresistible potentiality. If art is "fantastically deceitful and complex," then the terms of seducing girl-children and keeping them in thrall in the midst of mid-century America offer to Humbert a thrilling artistic possibility, a problem that, like bullfighting or mountain-climbing, involves not only the artistry but the safety of the protagonist. The measure of his skill is his survival.

Once again, vulnerability reminds us of value, and Nabokov is careful to keep Humbert's vulnerability before us in several different ways. Humbert is constantly reminding us of his former spells of insanity, and he fears that a more lasting dissociation is imminent. Nabokov also afflicts him with a heart disease that finally carries him off, a medical condition *ex machina* that is visited upon Nabokov's heroes roughly as often as its analogue, impotence or homosexuality, is visited upon his villains. Insanity, cardiac seizure, and prison provide the dangers, the abyss, the black velvet backdrop; but the narrative interest derives mainly from the comic impersonation that Humbert's situation forces him to give, the "deceit" we see acted out before us. Describing Quilty's tantalizing "cryptogrammic paper chase," Humbert doesn't miss the application of Quilty's performance to his own career as imposter: "We all admire the spangled acrobat with classical grace meticulously walking his tight rope in the talcum light; but how much rarer art there is in the sagging rope expert wearing scarecrow clothes and impersonating a grotesque drunk! *I* should know" (251).

Humbert always offers us a double vision of things in consequence of his impersonation within the philistine milieu. He is an imposter, the spy, the alien, with an imposter's life-and-death awareness of vulnerability. The intensity of his attention to the threats surrounding him gives to his voice and observations a pattern and coherence that are lacking in the observations in, say, *The Gift,* where no dramatic or narrative necessity aligns every particular in accordance with the larger meanings of the novel, and where Fyodor's voice is almost perfectly equivalent to Nabokov's own. The fusion in *Lolita* of the whole elegant, tender, comic Nabokovian voice with a Nabokovian favorite who yet spins his own fate out of his own perverse character, choices, and desires, creates, I believe, a "perfect monster"; and only in this novel has Nabokov been able to make the most of all the elements with which he habitually works. The double sense of Humbert's subjective fantasy—nympholepsy—and the objective world, which this obsession must depend upon for its prey and yet mimic for its survival, is the source of the novel's extraordinary narrative interest.

"I am ready to believe that the sensations I derived from natural fornication were much the same as those known to normal big males consorting with their normal big mates in that routine rhythm which shakes the world. The trouble was that those gentlemen had not, and I *had,* caught glimpses of an incomparably more poignant bliss. The dimmest of my pollutive dreams was a thousand times more dazzling than all the adultery the most virile writer of genius or the most talented impotent might imagine. My world was split. I was aware of not one but two sexes, neither of which was mine; both would be termed female by the anatomist." [20]

The objective world—a Riviera beach, a Parisian prostitute, the burghers of Ramsdale, an Arizona motel, Beardsley School, and so on—is not merely a kind of no-man's-land to Humbert's erotic fantasies, although this objective world constantly threatens him with its laws and prisons. Humbert's eroticism is bound to the denizens of this world. Lolita and her likes are wholly of it, bred of it, composed of it, a continuation of its characteristics, tinctures, and essence:

What drives me insane is the twofold nature of this nymphet—of every nymphet, perhaps; this mixture in my Lolita of tender dreamy childishness and a kind of eerie vulgarity, stemming from the snub-nosed cuteness of ads and magazine pictures, from the blurry pinkness of adolescent maidservants in the Old Country (smelling of crushed daisies and sweat); and from very young harlots disguised as children in provincial brothels; and then again, all this gets mixed up with the exquisite stainless tenderness seeping through the musk and the mud, through the dirt and the death, oh God, oh God. And what is most singular is that she, *this* Lolita, *my* Lolita, has individualized the writer's ancient lust, so that above and over everything there is—Lolita. [46–47]

Lolita is inseparable from her environment, just as Charlotte is, and as Richard Schiller, Quilty, and Pratt are. They are all at home in a manner in which Humbert, or any artist, can never be. And yet, Lolita is unaware of the magic of her own existence. Humbert, the artist, the pearl diver, moving through the habitat

of nymphets in a fragile bubble of mimicry, is the only consciousness in the novel capable of experiencing all that beauty, and his
tale is, in that sense, a hymn to both sensuous and sensual beauty
that would have simply wasted its sweetness if not for his transforming artistic consciousness. Many times it is only his fantasy,
only his heightened sensibility that make magic of the essence of
a scene. Notice the insistence on the complete subjectivity in the
following representative passage—it comes after what is perhaps
the novel's most erotic scene, Humbert's secret masturbation on
Lolita's coltish young legs:

> I felt proud of myself. I had stolen the honey of a spasm without
> impairing the morals of a minor. Absolutely no harm done. The
> conjurer had poured milk, molasses, foaming champagne into a
> young lady's new white purse; and lo, the purse was intact. Thus
> had I delicately constructed my ignoble, ardent, sinful dream; and
> still Lolita was safe—and I was safe. What I had madly possessed
> was not she, but my own creation, another, fanciful Lolita—per-
> haps, more real than Lolita; overlapping, encasing her; floating
> between me and her, and having no will, no consciousness—indeed,
> no life of her own. [64]

Here the fantastic and private world of Humbert's sexuality
briefly makes use of the objective world. Humbert, by integrating
the two worlds at least for a moment, is able to make from the union
his "own creation, another fanciful Lolita—perhaps more real
than Lolita." It is the casting aside of this solipsism that forms the
novel's moral pivot.

In one passage in *Pnin,* Victor plans a painting of an automobile. There is a curious and haunting image in this passage
that is extremely suggestive in terms of Nabokov's own work. "In
the chrome plating [of an automobile], in the glass of a sun-
rimmed headlamp, he would see a view of the street and himself
comparable to the microcosmic version of a room (with a dorsal

view of diminutive people) in that very special and very magical small convex mirror that, half a millenium ago, Van Eyck and Petrus Christus and Memling used to paint into their detailed interiors, behind the sour merchant or the domestic Madonna" (97).

The "very special and very magical" little mirror that Nabokov has painted into *Lolita*,[6] which gathers into its quicksilver microcosm the essence of the novel, is Humbert's description of Quilty's playlet *The Enchanted Hunters*:[7]

[Six out of the seven human hunters] went through a complete change of mind in Dolly's Dell, and remembered their real lives only as dreams or nightmares from which little Diana had aroused them; but a seventh Hunter (in a *green* cap, the fool) was a Young Poet, and he insisted, much to Diana's annoyance, that she and the entertainment provided (dancing nymphs, and elves, and monsters) were his, the Poet's, invention. I understand that finally, in utter disgust at this cocksureness, barefooted Dolores was to lead check-trousered Mona to the paternal farm behind the Perilous Forest to prove to the braggard she was not a poet's fancy, but a rustic, down-to-brown-earth lass—and a last-minute kiss was to enforce the play's profound message, namely, that mirage and reality merge in love.
[203]

Mrs. Richard Schiller, "pale and polluted and big with another's child," is, of course, analogous to the "down-to-brown-earth" lass whom the "Poet"—Humbert's analogue—discovers to have been hidden inside his imaginative construction, his object, all along. Humbert's erotic fantasizing seems only to have created a Lolita "more real" than Dolores Haze, and it is his imagination that is responsible for the semimythological young siren. But the motion of the novel, like the moral direction of Quilty's little play, is toward a discovery of the real-life human beings within those bubbles of fantasy. Mrs. Richard Schiller's humanity finally penetrates to Humbert in the Coalmont confrontation scene: "I could not kill *her,* of course, as some have thought. You see, I loved her. It was love at first sight, at last sight, at ever and ever sight" (272), Humbert tells us. His fantasties have hurt her, have ignored all human consequences, but at last he understands the moral evil of trying to make his sexual fantasies replace Lolita's "down-to-brown-earth" factuality. And this recognition makes his love beautiful.

Humbert's vision, and the voice in which he expresses this vision, are always illuminating the objective world with his own special fantasies. Just as in all of Nabokov's work, the objective world of commonsense must be transformed if it cannot be escaped.

A survey of Nabokov's work will reveal that reality, without an imaginative other world—philosophy, memory, art, chess, poetry, madness—to extend it, is everywhere presented to us as unbearable. All of Nabokov's favorites are engaged in processes that re-create reality, turn it into art, poetry, chess problems, nympholepsy (which is also an escape from *time*), the spinning of a "Zembla" that can be found on no map, a final flight to the bosom of one's creator in the case of Krug, a dismissal of the dreams we are made of and a walk off the preposterous stage-set for Cincinnatus.

In Humbert's case, a clinical argument could at least be extended to account for his aberration—the death of his young love before consummation. But this would account only for the sexuality in the relief the adult Humbert seeks in girl children; it cannot account for his desire to escape from time and death into that "great rosegrey never-to-be-had." Everywhere in Nabokov it is the fact of existence itself which must somehow be dealt with. We know of no good reason why Kinbote—or perhaps his name is "Botkin"—should have gone mad. We do not know from external circumstances why the protagonist in the short story "Lance"[8] is mad and fantasizes a space voyage. No particular reasons are offered for the young man's madness in the story "Signs and Symbols,"[9] we only learn that the world is a "hive of evil" whose threats drive him to suicide. Luzhin's fatal fantasies are baseless, causeless malignancies. We learn that Krug, in external circumstances successful, loving, and healthy, has been digging a subjective "pit of pure smiling madness" for years simply because he can find no answers. Aqua Veen is magically mad and dreams of "Terra the Fair"—another world. In Nabokov's work, fact kills, fantasy gives life.

Humbert's fantasy, his superimposition of his magical and private vision on the world around him, transforms everything. Humbert is not recording America but transforming it for us through the tinted lenses of his magical perversion. This sense of the objective surface made magical by the subjective imagination not only illuminates things outside Humbert; it also shows how Humbert sees himself flawlessly acting out his role of American daddy while deep in enemy territory. The possibilities that Humbert senses do not really reside in America or America's roles but behind the façade. These possibilities, not its own intrinsic merit, are what makes the façade interesting or amusing. By telling the story from Humbert's vantage, Nabokov allows all facts to become tinted with Humbert's subjective magic. If the story had been narrated omnisciently, the pathetic irony in the contrast between the world's fact and Humbert's fantasy would have been a great deal more difficult to deal with, for the omniscient voice would necessarily alert us to Humbert as pitiable object, and his fantasy would become as obtrusive as the chill drabness of the life it transforms.

When we are taken inside Lance or Kinbote's fantasy, we witness important experiences of depth and feeling; we "really are" along on Lance's intrepid voyage, although it takes place only inside his skull, and the love and loss Kinbote feels for Zembla seem to us a real experience. But outside those fantasies, when we are sharing the experience of Lance's parents or when Shade speaks to us around Kinbote by calling the madman a "fellow poet" who is only "turning a new leaf with the left hand," we are reminded bluntly of the smallness and meanness of the brute fact and the pathos of the fantasy which tries to surmount it, of the sterility that the raw fact and the unilluminated circumstance present. First-person narration by a fantast can have, of course, a pathos that is real enough; but the madman's voice need never express it *directly,* and this phenomenon necessarily alters our reaction to the fiction.

Humbert is a great deal more sane than Kinbote, but Nabokov has taken pains to touch Humbert's voice with an obsession and an illegitimate ecstasy that give a crazy zest and bumptiousness to his presentation of America. Humbert's sense of himself as alien and impostor lends an ironic verve to his extended impersonation of a genteel American daddy; the more "innocent" the milieu, the more suitable he finds it as a setting for his erotic fantasies, because the sensual thrills he can derive only from girl children are partially an escape from time, and the trappings of innocence are, of course, inevitably the trappings of the young. Some of Humbert's most thrilling moments are imaginatively connected with Lolita as a schoolgirl:

At one of [the desks], my Lolita was reading the chapter on "Dialogue" in Baker's *Dramatic Technique,* and all was very quiet, and there was another girl with a very naked, porcelain-white neck and wonderful platinum hair, who sat in front reading too, absolutely lost to the world and interminably winding a soft curl around one finger, and I sat beside Dolly just behind that neck and that hair, and unbuttoned my overcoat and for sixty-five cents plus the permission to participate in the school play, had Dolly put her inky, chalky, red-knuckled hand under the desk. Oh, stupid and reckless of me, no doubt, but after the torture I had been subjected to, I simply had to take advantage of a combination that I knew would never occur again. [200]

The novel is a *tour de force* for Humbert's voice, which of course expresses Humbert's sexuality, Humbert's flight from time and death, Humbert's mimicry, Humbert's moral metamorphosis. The monstrosity of the narrator Humbert and his solipsism, unlike Kinbote's, are not disconnected from the real world—they triumphantly transform that world and its commonplaces into a stage-set fraught with erotic potentialities and thrilling dangers, engaging Humbert himself and through him the reader in the narrative.

But perhaps because a "possible" life for Humbert and Lolita together is impossible to imagine—she is, remember, quite at home as a semiliterate Mrs. Richard Schiller living in a shack and the love of her life was the disgusting Quilty, not Humbert— Nabokov must find his means of closure for the tale in a massive administration of nothing less than death. Unlike the comic-hideous bloodbath in which Quilty and all that he represents in Humbert expires, this death is the "neat enjambment" and "melodic fall" that Nabokovian creations undergo when Nabokov desires closure and finality at the expense of verisimilitude. Only a fairytale could contain all the opportune deaths we have in *Lolita* and yet make them esthetically acceptable: Annabel; Humbert's mother; Charlotte; Lolita; Lolita's still-born girl baby; Humbert, another aging swan dead of Nabokov's cardiac syndrome; Quilty, the "dodo" aspect of Humbert, awash in a comic Niagara of gore and purgation. Everybody in the foreground dies unnaturally, and even a supernumerary like Charlie, Lolita's first love at Camp Q, is killed in the Korean War—perhaps proving that mortals should stay away from the precious and beautiful but ultimately death-dealing radium of fairytales.

Nabokov told Alfred Appel, "I think that what I would welcome at the close of a book of mine is a sensation of its world receding in the distance and stopping somewhere there suspended."[10] This mysterious and moving tranquility is more fully achieved in the great fairytale *Lolita* than anywhere else in his work.

6

Ada

Nabokov's World

Nabokov has written his own blurb for this large, ambitious, and uneven novel; it appears in the book's last paragraphs and recapitulates with partisan gusto the features of the work: "In spite of the many intricacies of plot and psychology, the story proceeds at a spanking pace," we are assured, and the blurb ends with a reminder of "a pretty plaything stranded among the forget-me-nots of a brook" (589). Nabokov's ideal reader—hyperattentive, insomniac, and possessing a microfilm memory—will, of course, recall the "pretty plaything" stranded among the brookside flowers about halfway through the novel: it is one of Van Veen's condoms, a "transparent, tubular thing, not unlike a sea-squirt, that had got caught in its downstream course in a fringe of forget-me-nots, good name, too" (275). This in microcosm is *Ada*'s manner; compared with *Lolita* or *Bend Sinister,* the novel is unfocused and erratic. It is also a bumptious, mannered, self-referential encyclopedia, and frequently seems to represent an attempt on Nabokov's part to satisfy a series of private fantasies. In a sense *Ada* is the most "pure" book Nabokov has written, for despite the assurances that the story maintains a "spanking pace" (the pace is in fact sometimes geological), the narrative elements have been subordinated to other, more idiosyncratic interests, the narrative tension on the plane of the fictional characters has been diminished, and the "clash" between writer and reader is the primary source of the novel's appeal. This is the Nabokov novel that demands the Nabokov *specialist:* a reader with sympathy, access to a good library, and a great deal of time. Unfortunately, it does not quite deserve this special attention, for it is, I think, despite some impressive writing, a very imperfect book.

Ada is divided into five parts, vastly unequal both qualitatively and quantitatively: part one, a long, sunny, beautifully written, cloying, and elegantly erotic account of Van Veen and his sister Ada's love affair (he is fourteen, she is twelve) at the family estate of Ardis, occupies the better half of the book; but part five, in which Van and Ada are now a shriveled ninety-seven and ninety-five, respectively, takes up only a score of pages. The middle parts, inferior to Nabokov's best writing, describe their separation, Van's own philosophical work *Texture of Time,* a great deal of hectic fornication, the suicide of Van and Ada's half-sister Lucette, plus assorted duels and deaths, punctuated by authorial didactics.

The tone of much of the book is soured not only by the unpleasantness of Van and Ada—both are dilettante snobs, and even Nabokov admits them to be "rather horrible people"[1]—but by the exaggerated predilections, mannerisms, and prejudices of Nabokov himself. The reference to the condom in the blurb exemplifies the mock-naughty humor that is so pervasive in *Ada.* To try to give vitality to the tone, Nabokov subjects us to several descriptions of young Van's "structurally perfect" stools, to the "fudge" of a ninety-seven-year-old's excrement, and to such embarrassing attempts at fun as the following passage: "As if doing his best to avail himself of his body, soon to be removed like a plate wherefrom one collects the last sweet crumbs, he now prized such small indulgences as squeezing out the vermicule of a black-head, or obtaining with the long nail of his little finger the gem of an itch from the depths of his left ear . . . or permitting himself what [an old family retainer] used to brand as *le plaisir anglais*—holding one's breath, and making one's own water, smooth and secret, while lying chin-deep in one's bath" (517).

Both Nabokov and his agent Van try to impress us with their heroics of deed and perception, but the results are unconvincing. For example, one of Van's boy-millionaire projects is a string of elaborate whorehouses called "Venus Villas," a franchise operation not unworthy of (or more imaginative than) the collective fantasies issuing from a midnight bull session of fraternity sophomores. Consider the fate of the one male prostitute retained in one of the clubs: "Two exceptionally sportive courtesans, entertaining Van, prevailed upon him one night to try the boy. . . . The little fellow could not disguise a state of acute indigestion, marked by unappetizing dysenteric symptoms that coated [Van's] shaft with mustard and blood, the result, no doubt, of eating too many green apples. Eventually, he had to be destroyed or given away" (355).

And when Van jealously discovers, in the middle of the book, that Ada's lover is a consumptive composer named Philip Rack, he insults an army captain simply to provoke a duel with a healthy adult male.[2]

He feels "keen exhilaration" as he prepares for the encounter. "Designing and re-designing various contingencies pertaining to that little duel might be compared to those helpful hobbies which polio patients, lunatics and convicts are taught by generous institutions, by enlightened administrators, by ingenious psychiatrists —such as bookbinding, or putting blue beads into the orbits of dolls made by other criminals, cripples and madmen" (307). That "keen exhilaration" is a formula from the nineteenth-century novel which can no longer convey authentic emotion, and the invitation to scorn those "criminals, cripples, and madmen" shows the lack of compassion of both Nabokov and Van, who share a mock-Satanic pose toward almost everything outside their own interests in this novel.

Van's first sexual experience is related in a tone that sets one's teeth on edge. We are invited vicariously to enjoy a "fat little wench" along with "our hell-raker" (this vocabulary is entirely characteristic), and Van's seigneurial contempt for this girl is unattractive. "He knew she was nothing but a fubsy pig-pink whorelet and would elbow her face away when she attempted to kiss him after he had finished and was checking with one quick hand . . . if his wallet was still in his hip pocket" (33).

Alfred Appel, Jr., loyally trying to separate Nabokov from his favorite, claims that Van's "ego is seen as the monster it often is, calmly and coldly transfixed by an anti-Freudian writer who offers no redeeming causation."[3] But not only is there no "redeeming causation," there is an effort throughout the novel to awe the reader with Van's intelligence, bravery, sexual powess (he is represented as having "sampled" more than two-hundred women), as well as his money, wit, ancestry, Hotspur recklessness, rake-hell vitality, and so on.

Robert Alter is cautious, to say the least, when he says that "the excess of perfection that [Van and Ada] must sustain makes them less interesting individually, less humanly engaging, than many of Nabokov's previous protagonists."[4] They are, in fact, stylized fantasy-figures.

We are assured by an overvoice that isn't quite Van's or Ada's (Van is intermittently supposed to be writing his memoirs with Ada's help, but Nabokov doesn't sustain this theme and loses interest for great stretches in the by-play of marginal notes between Van and Ada) that the two of them were a "unique,

super-imperial couple" who shared "prodigious individual awareness and young genius," and that the details of their affair,
expressed as it is in their superimperial prose, "must seem un-
pleasantly peculiar to peasants because detail is all."

"Our" young hell-raker fights duels and exposes card sharks,
he wins shipboard table-tennis matches, and is a "College Blue"
in football and cricket. He is also, of course, a "first-rate chess
player" and at thirty-five wins an endowed chair as professor at
Kingston University. When Van is scuffling with another of Ada's
lovers, Count Percy de Prey, Nabokov gives his superimperial
young genius precisely the kind of "satisfaction" we would expect
from boys' fiction: "Almost at once the Count's bursting face was
trapped in the crook of Van's arm. . . . [Soon] Percy lay pant-
ing like a dying gladiator, both shoulder blades pressed to the
ground by his tormentor, whose thumbs now started to manipulate horribly that heaving thorax" (275).

And the obligatory duel scene, whose antecedents are described
in terms of social class ("the kind of single combat described by
most Russian novelists and by practically all Russian novelists of
gentle birth"), is not meant as a parody, since it has no comic,
and hence anticlimactic, twist. It is played straight, and the
humor is, alas, unintentional:

[Van] felt the jolt of the bullet ripping off, or so it felt, the entire
left side of his torso. He swayed, but regained his balance, and with
nice dignity discharged his pistol in the sun-hazy air. . . .

The Captain strolled up and muttered rather gloomily: "I bet
you are in no condition to continue, are you?"

"I bet you can't wait—" began Van: he intended to say: "you
can't wait to have me slap you again," but happened to laugh on
"wait" and the muscles of mirth reacted so excruciatingly that he
stopped in mid-sentence and bowed his sweating brow.   [311]

Shakespeare makes chivalric bravado work with Mercutio, but

Mercutio does not *laugh,* and his wit is grim and realistic: "No, 'tis not so deep as a well, nor so wide as a church door; but 'tis enough, 'twill serve. . . . They have made worms' meat of me." Nabokov's "mirth" is far wide of the mark, and laughter is ridiculous. What is Van supposed to be laughing at? The artificiality of the passage is embarrassing.

Speaking of the constant journalistic attacks on his father in "the reactionary press," Nabokov relates that, when he was about twelve (the best age for enjoying boys' fiction, obviously), "the most powerful of the Rightist newspapers employed a shady journalist to concoct a scurrilous piece containing insinuations that my father could not let pass. Since the well-known rascality of the actual author of the article made him 'non-duelable' (*neduelesposobniy,* as the Russian dueling code had it), my father called out the somewhat less disreputable editor of the paper in which the article had appeared."[5]

In creating his Van Veen, Nabokov has evidently skimmed the fantasies from his own adolescence as well as those of Pushkin. Van is a veritable baron, a millionaire, and a Byronic-Luciferian figure, and the narrative becomes only a series of unconvincing triumphs on his part. Right after the duel, wounded Van is taken to a hospital; "his first reaction" there is to demand a private room "where heartbroken kings had tossed in transit" (312). Thus, by making the reflexes of a snob ascendent over common recuperation, Nabokov violates good sense and rudimentary psychology. But Van is, after all, the scholar who "liked to change his abode at the end of a section or chapter or even paragraph" (365). He finally makes it impossible for the reader to have any real sense of participation in his story. Thus Nabokov pays a bone-breaking price simply to assert some long-dormant juvenilia.

But Van is not a fictional character in the primary sense, nor is the key to understanding the novel to view it as a narrative, or judge it with the standards of mimetic realism. The world of Antiterra—it was aptly labeled by *Time* magazine as an "ever-ever land"—is nothing less than a complete heart's-desire construction. It is, simply, the happily-ever-after portion of Nabokov's lifelong attempt to create out of his art a fairytale, and the only villain that survives in it is time itself. No other source of tension is allowed to be potent. Van Veen is thus not an objectively realized character, he is a mask: it is not an accident that the initials "V.V." often replace the name "Van Veen," for the "V.V." is also Vladimir Vladimirovich, Nabokov himself.

The science-fiction aspect of the world-as-Antiterra is sustained only insofar as it will lend itself to Nabokov's fantasizing: it bears approximately the same resemblance to our world that a donnishly annotated Jules Verne novel does, and its little jokes on matters of public knowledge in our world are uniformly (and significantly) harmless. Thus, Mississippi is ruled by Negroes; Chekov's masterwork is *The Four Sisters;* one catches only thirty-nine winks in a nap; Oxford is a women's college; a belted raincoat is a "garbotosh"; duels are sometimes fought on Boston Common; England annexed France in 1815; the *New Yorker* is *The Beau and the Butterfly;* English stiff-upper-lip character is formed on the fabled playing fields of an exclusive prep school called "Note"; America and Russia are a single nation, geologically and linguistically joined.

But these scraps of humor are, finally, quite marginal, for the significant alterations performed on terrestrial reality and history allow Nabokov to manipulate his Antiterran world into precisely the realm his imagination requires for its "ever-ever" land; his Antiterrans have been set free as Krug or Pnin or Humbert can never be.

The imaginariness of this world is useful in a different sense from, say, that of Krug's homeland. In *Bend Sinister,* the imaginariness serves several functions, but it does not relieve the Nazi horrors on which it draws for its terror. In fact, the imaginariness of that land and that history allows Krug the historical innocence which makes his resistance to Paduk's regime morally admissible and credible. He cannot really believe David is in danger if he does not know about Auschwitz. Further, it allows Nabokov to magnify the preposterous for savage and comic comment, as in the confrontation between Paduk and Krug; and its *obvious* artificiality renders the very revelation of that artificiality meaningful. At the end of the novel, Nabokov dissolves the world he has created. The gesture is convincing and effective because we know the imaginariness of that world; a "real" world cannot be so readily dismissed.

But *Ada* and Antiterra are intended to function in another manner. They do not exist to make comments on the real world, as do the artificial worlds of *Bend Sinister, Invitation to a Beheading, 1984, Gulliver's Travels, Brave New World,* or even lesser-known but equally didactic constructs like E. M. Forster's beehive society in "The Machine Stops." Antiterra's lure is that it is demonstrably a much more compatible place than our world for a male sensibility of great gifts, Edwardian tastes, and *ancien régime* ancestry. It is unique in that there, at long last, harm is not the norm, nor is human history what Pnin characterizes as "the history of pain." It is, at last, an "ever-ever" land. Or at least *almost* one: time, the omnivorous enemy, is still unbanishable.

Astrophysicists with a statistical bent have estimated that the cosmos is so populous that the odds on there *not* being another world exactly like ours are a billion to one; if time is seen as yet another medium in which to predicate such a statistical probability, the odds are replaced by something near "certainty"—and this is the philosophical tenet on which Nabokov plays in his creation.

The alterations[6] Nabokov has made seem slight at first glance: only a telescoping of the *fin-de-siècle* and Edwardian eras into a later portion of the twentieth-century, where the iron curtain finds it equivalent in a gold curtain and the Soviet Union and China are a huge and menacing Tartary. The world seems still ours, with only a few minor discrepancies of history and science; but the effect on Nabokov's imagination of this liberation from the ugly facts of terrestrial history is marked. In the reconstruction of history and geography, of war and peace, nasty episodes like the Russian Revolution have been carefully omitted, while favorites like Shakespeare, Proust, H. G. Wells' *Invisible Man,* Marvell, Rimbaud, Rembrandt, Joyce, Turgenev, Keats, Jane Austen are seemingly unaffected; and an American novelist can still give us a *Chiron* (Updike's *The Centaur*), Browning is still almost himself as Brown, and if Chekov's sisters have added a fourth, the play is still almost a masterpiece.

If the larger patterns of history are still a "beastly farce" in this ever-ever land, all of Nabokov's private interests achieve public importance. In the historical sector, we find the world is spared the burden of nuclear energy—at least the word is deemed meaningless in a Scrabble game, and Van has to settle for "unclear" instead. But nothing more is made of this momentous unburdening. Some mysterious "L-disaster" has made electricity[7] itself illegal and un-available ("its very name having become a 'dirty word' among upper-upper-class families . . . to which the Veens . . . happened to belong"). But Nabokov, uninterested in a fiction dealing with public fact, substitutes some obscure use of water as a medium for convenient phone calls and ignores the contribution electricity makes to the workings of internal combustion engines. Thus his Antiterran "facts" are casually rearranged or ignored when inconvenient; airplanes and telephones are there when needed, and no nonsense such as government, revolution, or race is allowed to intrude far enough into the Veenish world to deserve more than a mention.

But not all of the changes from Terra to Antiterra, the shifts that make things preposterous to Nabokov preposterous to every Antiterran (it is, after all, *his* world), are even as significant as these. In fact, matters of great historical importance are summarized in a line or shrugged aside, and matters of private importance are magnified. Nabokov uses Antiterra to settle several old scores, largely cultural, bookish, and idiosyncratic in nature. Thus, in a world where "artists are the only gods," Van can inherit with his lease the discarded works of "Faulknermann" (Shade was seen dumping Faulkner out, too, and "Death in Venice" is Nabokov's special choice as definitive mock-culture). On Antiterra, Swinburne becomes "Burning Swine"; Steinbeck's *Travels with Charley* becomes "Old Beckstein's *Tabby;* Freud's agent is a "Dr. Sig Heiler"; Lowell and Auden are jammed into "Lowden, a minor poet and translator"; and Osberg (Borges) is dismissed as a creator of "pretentious fairy tales." Mlle. Larivière, whose Maupassant story is analyzed as obviously silly and unsound (the unfortunates in *The Necklace* would have been scrupulous to check on the necklace's cost before committing themselves to their lifetime of redeeming drudgery), wins the "Lebon" Prize for Literature, the proper noun supposedly devalued as well as decoded if we read it in a mirror.

But the artist who receives the roughest treatment is T. S. Eliot, a contemporary of Nabokov, whose effect on twentieth-century terrestrial sensibility is antithetically mirrored on Antiterra. First we hear of some Veen property sold to "Mr. Eliot, a Jewish businessman" (5), a reference to Eliot's supposedly anti-Semitic bent and the correct Dantesque reincarnation. He next comes before us as a kind of fissioned presence, as both the cigar-chomping "real estate magnate Milton Eliot" and "Kithar K. L. Sween, who wrote verse" (459). These strange presences—Sween is "author of *Agonic Lines*" (*Sweeney Agonistes*)—are soon seen "comparing cigars," obviously a hyper-philistine activity, and we again glimpse Sween "lunching with a young fellow who sported a bullfighter's sideburns and other charms" (465), an innuendo about homosexuality. Eliot and "Kithar" are again together in the final blast, and Sween is now a "banker who at sixty-five had become an avant-garde author," and who "in the course of one miraculous year . . . had produced *The Waistline*, a satire in free verse on Anglo-American feeding habits, and *Cardinal Grishkin*, an overtly subtle yarn extolling the Roman faith. The poem was but the twinkle in an owl's eye; as to the novel it had already been pronounced 'seminal' by celebrated young critics . . . who lauded it in reverential voices pitched so high that an ordinary human ear could not make much of that treble volubility; it seemed, however, all very exciting, [but] after a great bang of obituary essays . . . both the satire and the romance were . . . forgotten" (505–506).

This devaluation of Eliot's reputation is easily accomplished on Antiterra. The satisfactions of living there are evidently immediate and intense, at least for those with axes to grind.

But all mimetic and dramatic interest in *Ada* has been sacrificed to these semiprivate executions and other authorial intrusions. The situations in the novel are not convincing, and neither are the characters, with the exception of Aqua and Lucette, who are suicides, and Percy de Prey, who is killed in combat. Although the interest we take in the fate of fictional characters on a narrative plane is replaced to an extent by the interest we take in Nabokov's own genius, and in his ideas, opinions, and art—in

a novel, not even an artist as great as Nabokov can surrender his
hold on our empathy and all sources of simple narrative suspense
and find an adequate substitute for it. We have seen Nabokov
ignoring mimicry before—the tendency has always been there,
hindsight assures us—but never on such a scale and with such
heavy losses.

Van's father, Demon, for example, is seized by his creator as
brazenly as were those transient academics who furnished testimony to Krug's genius in *Bend Sinister:*

"If I could write," mused Demon, "I would describe, in too many
words no doubt, how passionately, how incandescently, how incestuously—*c'est le mot*—art and science meet in an insect, in a
thrush, in a thistle of that ducal bouquet. Ada is marrying an out-
door man, but her mind is a closed museum, and she, and dear
Lucette, once drew my attention, by a creepy coincidence, to certain details of that other triptych, that tremendous garden of
tongue-in-cheek delights, circa 1500, and, namely, to the butterflies
in it—a Meadow Brown, female, in the center of the right panel,
and a Tortoiseshell in the middle panel, placed there as if settled on
a flower—mark the 'as if,' for here we have an example of exact
knowledge on the part of those two admirable little girls, because
they say that actually the *wrong* side of the bug is shown, it should
have been the underside, if seen, as it is, in profile, but Bosch evidently found a wing or two in the corner cobweb of his casement
and showed the prettier upper surface in depicting his incorrectly
folded insect. I mean I don't give a hoot for the esoteric meaning,
for the myth behind the moth, for the masterpiece-baiter who makes
Bosch express some bosh of his time, I'm allergic to allegory and am
quite sure he was just enjoying himself by crossbreeding casual
fancies just for the fun of the contour and color, and what we have
to study, as I was telling your cousins, is the joy of the eye, the feel
and the taste of the woman-sized strawberry that you embrace *with*

him, or the exquisite surprise of an unusual orifice—but you are not following me, you want me to go, so that you may interrupt her beauty sleep, lucky beast! [436–437]

The statement is almost a précis of several enduring Nabokovian interests: the meeting of "art and science," of esthetics and necessity in Nature; the dismissal of "the myth behind the moth"—Nabokov loathes in all art any mythic, religious, or anthropological substratum (not coincidentally Eliot's most obvious source of extrinsic reference); the alliterative glissando ("allergic to allegory," "contour and color," "creepy coincidence); the indifference to real speech ("in depicting his incorrectly folded insect"); the refusal to ignore a minor subthematic line of thought ("incestuously—c'est le mot"), a refusal that bespeaks the author's egotistic eagerness to show his awareness of all the facets of an idea before the reader anticipates him; a precision of description and proper noun (Tortoiseshell, Meadow Brown) ill suited to the recollections of an aging roué and gambler, whose interests would seem to lie elsewhere.

The novel might well serve as a textbook for a course in Nabokov. It is intended to be a text, by Nabokov *on* Nabokov, and has dismissed all dramatic resources in order to be a text. But Nabokov insists on pretending that it is a novel, that these are its characters, and this is the way they talk, and his pretense compromises even the intrinsic interest of his observations. In *Pale Fire*, Nabokov's indifference to consistent mimicry has damaged the characterization of Kinbote, but that indifference is really a by-product of the author's moral distaste for the world of Gradus, and the displacement of Kinbote up the scale of authorial favoritism toward Shade is not allowed to become wholly debilitating; further, the plot of *Pale Fire* has compensatory melodramatic interests. But *Ada* is almost without conflict. It is naked Nabokoviana.

The Part and the Whole

The unequalness of Nabokov's interest in the part and his interest in the whole is nowhere more pronounced than it is in *Ada*. Van simply has too little to do, nothing to learn, and no need to change. Because time is his real antagonist and time is dramatically difficult, the lack of narrative tension is everywhere evident.

After hundreds of pages detailing events that took place in days or months, Nabokov compresses years of narrational time into a sentence; but this crumpling and compressing of time's structure can also crumple and compress verisimilitude, empathy, a sense of participation. Nabokov takes so little interest in the middle portions of Van's life that he even pretends they are devoid of all events. How much interest can we take in Van, our multimillionaire young hell-raker and *homme fatal*, how can he seem real, when Nabokov dismisses a fifth of his life in the following manner? "He spent in Kingston [University] a score of dull years (variegated by trips abroad), an obscure figure around which no legends collected in the university or the city. Unbeloved by his austere colleagues, unknown in local pubs, unregretted by male students, he retired in 1922, after which he resided in Europe" (507).

Parody in Nabokov's best work is, I have claimed, primarily a means of retaining an effect while indicating only a qualified approval of that effect. For example, Humbert's passionate love for Mrs. Richard Schiller is saved from mawkishness by touches of irony that restore an equilibrium and a sense of qualifying intelligence: " 'Good by-aye!' she chanted, my American sweet immortal dead love; for she is dead and immortal if you are reading this. I mean, such is the formal agreement with the so-called authorities" (282).

Nabokov himself analyzed his use of parody in somewhat the same manner: "While I keep everything on the very brink of parody, there must be on the other hand an abyss of seriousness, and I must make my way along this narrow ridge between my own truth and the caricature of it."[8]

But there is no ridge in *Ada,* no "abyss of seriousness" more palpable than time, and the touches of bookish parody are merely clever remarks, not gyroscopic necessities for stabilizing the tone. The novel's single most poignant and powerful emotional effect is produced—as it is always produced in Nabokov's work—by intensifying value through threat of loss. The author threatens whatever his favorites cherish: Pnin almost breaks his beloved crystal bowl from Victor; Humbert's love for Mrs. Richard Schiller is hopeless. In the same manner, Van and Ada's young love affair, by itself only hectic copulation, assumes a heart-stopping value because it is threatened by carnivore time. Van remembers from across decades that "when he grew too loud, she [Ada] shushed, shushingly breathing into his mouth, and now her four limbs were frankly around him as if she had been love-making for years in all our dreams—but impatient young passion (brimming like Van's over-flowing bath while he is reworking this, a crotchety gray old wordman on the edge of a hotel bed) did not survive the first few blind thrusts; it burst at the lip of the orchid" (121).

Unfortunately, however, most of the parody in *Ada* is inadequate to save from silliness the effect upon which it comments, or to save the author himself from accusations of caring more about his fantasies than about good fiction.

Speaking to the old family retainer Boutellian (lovable lecher and drunk, fiercely loyal to the Veens), it is not redemptive for Van to wisecrack to both Boutellian and us: "Quite the old comedy retainer, aren't you?" (159). Precisely, but merely

...ings to play with the notion of Terra, our world, as the
...ary, silly, vaguely sinister place he has been telling us it is
...lf a century:

...r Aqua, whose fancies were apt to fall for all the fangles of
...s and Christians, envisaged vividly a minor hymnist's paradise,
...ure America of alabaster buildings one hundred stories high,
...bling a beautiful furniture store crammed with tall white-
...ed wardrobes and shorter fridges. . . . She heard magic-music
...s talking and singing, drowning the terror of thought. . . .
...unmentionable magnetic power denounced by evil lawmakers
...his our shabby country . . . was used on Terra as freely as water
...air, as bibles and brooms. Two or three centuries earlier she
...ht have been just another consumable witch. [21]

...ice here the alliance of "cranks and Christians," the habitual
...erence to the "terror of thought" among the masses, the
...inishment implied by the linkage of "bibles and brooms," the
...erence to a "consumable witch." These statements are his
...enge on public history, common and communal fact. At long
...t, Nabokov has been able to set things right. Antiterra is, after
..., his world, and it is an improved version of ours.

...It is really within the shadow of madness, terror, and death
...at Nabokov's art works best; when he can afford to be extra-
...oral; and where he can allow himself interest and sympathy for
...onfavorites. His special genius seems to come to life when he
...an create upon a fatal fairytale vehicle a wonderfully real-
...eeming surface: for Nabokov is never realistic in his best work,
...e is fantastic, and his realism is not the authentic realistic artist's
...nterest in the way we live, the interest we find in concentrated
...orm in, say, a Flemish interior or the Army Air Corps of James
...Gould Cozzens' *Guard of Honor*, or even the ruminations of a
...Moses Herzog; Nabokov's is the interest of an artist whose vision
...always includes both the photographic realism of surface

mentioning this failure does not redeem it. And so, when Lucette
"returns the balled hanky of many an old romance to her bag"
(369); when we are informed that the "atmosphere of those new
trysts added a novelistic touch (Aleksey and Anna may have
asterisked here!)" (521); when a chance moment is itself
asterisked by the comment that "it was all, historically speaking,
at the dawn of the novel which was still in the hands of parsonage
ladies and French academicians" (127)—when any or all of
these parodic touches are underlined, they fail to modify our
reaction to what Nabokov is trying so desperately to make respectable. He makes acknowledgment that previous deities have
passed this way, but his acknowledgment does not constitute a
use of convention for comic effect in the manner of S. J. Perel-
man or any other great parodist, nor does the wit help control
the tone of what might be melodramatic if it were told without
irony. Since Van has nothing to learn, little to fear, and no
mistakes allowed him, his life simply lacks the makings of a long
novel.

Novelistic structure in *Ada* has been replaced by a succession of
tenuously related tableaux. Nabokov's intent has been to render
a kind of technicolor gorgeousness, and he uses his gifts for
stereoscopic description to create a world of fabulous *fin-de-
siècle* luxury. *Ada* contains something not found in Nabokov's
earlier work—descriptions of food; and just as in the works of a
nineteenth-century writer like Dickens, the food is used to generate a direct sense of good feeling, of rightness and good fortune,
of bounty. In keeping with this expansiveness, a great many of
the effects and scenes in *Ada* are opened up, elastically expanded,
as moments are in opera. There is a succession of lacquered and
annotated moments where time has been almost immobilized. An
instant of shared perception during Van and Ada's first summer
yields not only the doubleness of the metaphor at which they

independently arrive, but also a memory of that instant, which is reworked in the manuscript of an aging genius; and a moment of adolescent perception and experience is thus heightened by the application to it of twinned intelligence at the time of its occurrence, and by the comments that the "old gray wordman" and his wife make upon the memory.

Nabokov's freedom from the obligations of plot enables him to expand each effect at will. In consequence, we have never been so aware of his hand. Nor have the individual parts of one of his works ever had less organic relationship with one another. But by removing his art some distance from the brink of the abyss, Nabokov has crippled it: he needs that sense of fatality and melodrama breathing hot and close. It is only with episodic effects such as Aqua's suicide that the novel achieves something vivid and memorable, for just as in that poignant contrast between the sexual intercourse of scarcely formed adolescents and the "old gray wordman" trying desperately, with only his words, to give life everlasting to an incomparable instant, death creates value for all the riches of consciousness to which death puts an end.

Aqua's Madness and Death: the Magnified Moment

Aqua's place in the convoluted tale and family tree of the Veens is more complicated and obscure than that of any other character in the novel. Part of the complication and obscurity arise from Nabokov's arbitrary attempts to integrate her into the bloodlines and plot activity, where she has no viable function. Her real function, like Ophelia's in *Hamlet,* is to go mad and die.

Dan and Demon Veen are brothers, Aqua and Marina are sisters. Dan is married to Marina, Demon to Aqua. Aqua is "less pretty, and far more dotty, than Marina" (19), and Demon

prefers Marina to her sexually: in fact about manner that Ada and Van are and that Van was substituted for Dem child unbeknownst to Aqua. All this bu point. Nabokov wants Aqua in his nov derive from her madness and suicide and remarkably moving.

Rather too casually—almost as casually "once upon a time"—Nabokov begins his us that during Aqua's "fourteen years of m spent a broken series of steadily increasin riums" (19). We are off, our destination and Nabokov can make brilliant use of the i a melodramatic vehicle in motion. Many of terra and some of the novel's most powerful within the confines of Aqua's fate. With ou assured by Aqua's downhill velocity, Nabokov his magnifying glass at will. It is as if, once free tions of living with his characters—which in h involves making them favorites—Nabokov sympathy, interest, or affection which he oth these creatures. Nabokov and his narrator in "S couldn't approve of Nina unless she were going cause she is going to die, she becomes for them a and appealing character; we are free to enjoy vain and shoddy and silly as it is, as long as it difference. In this sense, Nabokov's use of fate, fat figuration of death allows him to feel, and to ma attachment that otherwise would violate his scrup moral, ethical, and intellectual valuation.

Nabokov, sure of his hold on the reader, uses

phenomena, and the mysteries within and behind. We never have the middleground alone, the world before us is never really enough. Escape is Nabokov's abiding interest. He is, in this sense, a sham realist, a fabulist disguising his fairytales as realism. That "dodo-like" creature was, after all, a swan, and it is the death of swans Nabokov has made his subject.

Aqua finally becomes "unwilling to suffer another relapse" from a period of relative sanity and peace; as usual, the world of evil from which the madman or suicide or fantast escapes is tainted by the group. A psychiatrist, always the object of Nabokov's purest loathing, is the master villain—for the psychiatrist, like Eric Wind smacking his lips over the word "group," has tried to enforce a group on Aqua, too. "A demented patient could outwit in one snap an imbecile pedant" (27), of course, and the pedant is not only an imbecile, he is the supreme Nazi, a "Dr. Sig Heiler."

Nabokov can even afford to make one of several references to his own work by including among Aqua's collection of suicide pharmaceuticals a pill we last saw Humbert administering to Lo at the Enchanted Hunters Hotel, a fat purple one full of "the grape-blood of emperors." And looking at it, Aqua is reminded of the essentially terrene story "in which the little gypsy enchantress in the Spanish tale (dear to Ladore schoolgirls) puts to sleep all the sportsmen and all their bloodhounds at the opening of the hunting season" (28). For each phrase in Aqua's statement we can substitute a complex of associations from *Lolita:* Lolita is a Spanish name; "gypsy" a romantic adjective used everywhere in Nabokov; the "schoolgirls" makes an obvious connection; putting to sleep is a form of enchantment; the "sportsmen" could refer to Humbert, and the "bloodhound"—not the usual kind of hunting dog, notice—of course refers to nemesis Quilty; and the "hunting season" is an obvious reference to Hotel, play, and theme. A great many of Nabokov's major preoccupations appear in *Ada* in similar full-blown allusive reincarnation.[9]

The quixotic gesture against the brutal executioners is also allowed Aqua: her suicide note mentions "psykitsch," in reference to Dr. Sig Heiler, whom he calls "Herr Doktor Heiler," evoking Germany, for just as with the third Bachofen sister at the Institute or Hagen or Quilty or Eric Wind, Germany is always part of the Nabokovian code for evil, and psychiatrists are its high priests. It is also characteristic that Aqua destroys herself (as Yasha did in "Triangle within Circle") with a good deal of bravery. The "psykitsch" group fatuously misses the point, for our fused psychiatrist-Hitler, "still in his baggy khaki shorts," can do nothing more than point out that "Sister" Aqua's body lies "as if buried prehistorically, in a *fetus-in-utero* position," a remark that seems "relevant" to his students. (28–29).

Despite all the score-settling and axe-grinding that Nabokov has packed into Aqua's tale, the terror, madness, and suicide are quite moving. Unlike the death that at last comes to hover behind favorites Van and Ada, Aqua's suicide induces a feeling of horror. It tears her out of the rational continuum of her life, and it has the arbitrariness of disease and even of the "broken promises" that the overvoice in *Bend Sinister* mentions as an attribute of the "nameless presence" that penetrates into Krug's life and finally extinguishes it. Death is horrifying to the extent it is untimely and wasteful; the Veens, like John Shade, are not subject to *meaningless* death. In their shriveled nineties, the Veens are going to be gently closed shut; they will endure only the "neat enjambment" and "melodic fall" proper to the death of poets, and we are informed that "our time-racked, flat-lying couple . . . would die, as it were, *into* the finished book, into Eden or Hades, into the prose of the book or the poetry of its blurb" (587). That is, they will be assumed into *Ada*'s fairytale artifice, as Shade is assumed into *Pale Fire* (the Veens are not coincidentally translating Shade's "famous poem" into Russian the last we see of them), or the way Lolita and her stillborn daughter are finally drawn back into the fairytale artifice of *Lolita,* carefully set back into its jeweler's cotton, finally laid to rest in velvet, under a taut-springed lid.

Early in *Ada* we are told that "no sooner did all the fond, all the frail, come into close contact with [Van] . . . than they were bound to know calamity, unless strengthened by a strain of his father's demon blood" (20), which is really to say that all the minor or secondary characters are subject to fatal strokes of authorial favoritism rather than enjoying a rational continuity. But once these characters have been marked for death, and once the death vehicle is in motion, once Nabokov is assured of our attention, he can present to us, without fear of being banal or commonplace or "vulgar," a more or less ordinary life suddenly become valuable simply because it is about to be extinguished. We recognize this with Nina in "Spring in Fialta"; and the parents of the young madmen in "Lance" and "Signs and Symbols" are allowed to come before us without genius, beauty, comic vulgarity, or monstrousness because they are marked for extinction, too, even if that extinction is psychic rather than physical death. Neither Nabokov nor his agent Humbert can really live with Lolita, but both of them can love her once they are assured that their attentions will not be prolonged past the moment in Coalmont when Mrs. Schiller's commonplace humanity causes Humbert's moral transformation. Loss, by definition, cannot be prolonged indefinitely, for then it stands the danger of becoming only life—that essentially "flattish and faded" and perhaps meaningless continuity that all favorites in Nabokov find impossible. Nabokov can only interest himself in the quotidian if he knows it cannot last.

Ada and Time

Not only does Nabokov include his own blurb for *Ada* within the text, he also insists on annotating every aspect of the book. The details, dialogue, and events that make up the narrative receive rhetorical and speculative attention from the overvoice and the characters themselves, who stand in an extremely privileged position in relation to the story of their own lives. The action is made doubly conscious of itself in this manner, and an aged Ada is there to edit the manuscript along with Van. Two old geniuses describing their shared young genius—a sufficiency of awareness, if nothing else. Thus, the novel's self-consciousness is raised almost exponentially, and this self-consciousness extends to its use of time. Time is both the mainspring of thematic tension and a speculative subject in *Ada*.

Nabokov has dismissed the middle portions of Van's and Ada's lives simply to superimpose those shriveled and agonized word-people, now merged as "Vaniada," on the demonically virile and healthy young "super-imperial" lovers they had been eighty years before. Just as *Lolita* becomes more poignant when we realize now and again it is a posthumous book (and posthumous in relation to both Humbert and his subject), and just as the shadow of death altered our experience with Nina in "Spring in Fialta," so *Ada* insists on that "abyss of seriousness" to serve as a velvet backdrop for its effects. The overvoice leaves little implicit, pointing out the effect for us: "One great difficulty. The strange mirage-shimmer standing in for death should not appear too soon in the chronicle and yet it should permeate the first amorous scenes. Hard but not insurmountable (I can do anything, I can tango and tap-dance on my fantastic hands)" (584).

The superimposition of youth and age is the novel's primary dramatic use of time: it is the carnivore in the forests of the

fairytale, the novel's only villainous force, the only force that
really cannot be "ruled." Remember that for Prospero, too, every
third thought will be of his own death. The magician who can
"tango and tap-dance" on his hands can trick gravity only for
a moment, and the personification of Thought-as-acrobat in
Bend Sinister comes back to us: those "aging, weakening hands"
are simply no match for the banal but unconquerable law of
gravity, rule of time, and triumph of death.

Not only is time used as backdrop to the tale of the Veens,
Van himself presents to us the essential speculative insights at
which he has arrived in his *Texture of Time,* and we can assume
Nabokov intends these insights to be taken with complete seriousness. He is advancing a thesis about time that I think he expects
to stand on its own as an extranarrative contribution to perceptual and metaphysical speculation.

Van-Nabokov is very perceptive in pointing out how our
metaphoric fallacy of time's "flowing," which uses a spatial con-
cept to describe time, might have been derived from our own
innate physical self-awareness: "We regard Time as a kind of
stream, [and] . . . end up by being unable to speak of Time
without speaking of physical motion. Actually, of course, the sense
of its motion is derived from many natural, or at least familiar,
sources—the body's innate awareness of its own bloodstream, the
ancient vertigo caused by rising stars, and, of course, our methods
of measurement, such as the creeping shadow line of a gnomon,
the trickle of an hourglass, the trot of a second hand—and here
we are back in Space" (540–541).

But Nabokov, however elegant his metaphysics and style, gets
himself into culs-de-sac with such comments as:

> At this point, I suspect, I should say something about my attitude
> to "Relativity." It is not sympathetic. What many cosmogonists
> tend to accept as an objective truth is really the flaw inherent in

mathematics which parades as truth. The body of the astonished person moving in Space is shortened in the direction of motion and shrinks catastrophically as the velocity nears the speed beyond which, by the fiat of a fishy formula, no speed can be. That is his bad luck, not mine—but I sweep away the business of his clock's slowing down. Time, which requires the utmost purity of consciousness to be properly apprehended, is the most rational element of life, and my reason feels insulted by those flights of Technology Fiction. One especially grotesque inference, drawn '(I think by Engelwein) from Relativity Theory—and destroying it, if drawn correctly—is that the galactonaut and his domestic animals, after touring the speed spas of Space, would return younger than if they had stayed at home all the time. [543]

Unfortunately for Nabokov, he can no more dismiss the theory of relatively by calling Einstein "Engelwein" than the Inquisition could preserve the Ptolemaic Universe by the burning of Bruno: the interchange between matter and energy that takes place as a body's speed approaches that of light is no more subject to an amateur's insults than is the thump of Newton's apple; it is a fact provable any and every day in hundreds of laboratories and their cyclotrons, and no one, no matter how purely he wants to perceive time, can "sweep away" relativity. It is not a "fishy formula"; it is illogical but true. Ada, at least, may be right when she tells Van that, as for time, "our senses are simply not meant to perceive it."

Nabokov's gesture, however, is useful to the reader. It shows again how powerfully Nabokov desires to dismiss from *his* world everything that is esthetically inadmissible. The energy of this desire runs throughout all his fiction.

The relative failure of the novel seems to me to stem from Nabokov's insistence on fidelity to his fantasies rather than to dramatic and narrative obligations. We are asked to join him in his "dream-bright America"—and it is no accident that Ada marries a man named Vinelander, "whose fabulous ancestor discovered our country"—but his America proves to be as "flattish and faded" as Humbert finds things after he has killed off Quilty. There are no real sources of tension available to a narrative artist who not only foregoes suspense but also takes little interest in the moral burdens of middleground life or in money, marriage, institutions, commonsense psychology, technology fiction, and the like. In one hasty sentence, Nabokov summarizes enormous stretches of Van and Ada's lives. These stretches of life and time are the ones that the rest of us inhabit, and Nabokov is not interested in them. He never has been.

But then, all his other fairytales are much more like the Grimms' than like Andersen's (the "bedside Dane," as Nabokov calls him in *Lolita*); Arcady is not a very interesting or convincing place, even if it resembles pre-Revolutionary Russia, and sex is not very real if the participants are "hell-rakers" and nymphomaniacs. Nabokov, whose art works best under tension, damages his narrative badly when he reduces the evils of history to a clever narrational paradox, when eating asparagus with the fingers, for example, evokes "the reformed 'sign of the cross' for protesting against which (a ridiculous little schism measuring an inch or so from thumb to index) so many Russians had been burnt by other Russians only two centuries earlier on the banks of the Great Lake of Slaves" (259).

The flaw in *Ada* is that it is perhaps too much Nabokov's world. Where is the conflict and the suspense, the "abyss"? One can only hope Prospero will grow bored in Milan and row back for his Caliban: stories, especially long ones, should be written about unhappy monsters, not overachieving wizards.

7

Epilogue: "The Ballad of
Longwood Glen"

In his fiction Nabokov is always concerned with both a world and a world apart, with an objective reality on which we can more or less agree ("There is no Zembla") and a consciousness which creates a subjective world of its own ("There is not only a Zembla, but I am its king"). The conflict between these two worlds may be that between art and life, as in *Bend Sinister,* or that between the present and the past, as in *Pnin.* The extremely complex relationship of these two sets of realities is the mark of Nabokov's most advanced fiction; earlier European fiction like *King, Queen, Knave* does not employ it, or employs it, as in *Despair,* in a comparatively simple fashion. The idea reaches its apotheosis in *Ada,* where the world is wholly reimagined, and it is our Terra that is the dream—or the nightmare.

The real complexities of Nabokov's art lie in the grazing, mirroring, adjacent planes of objective and subjective "realities," and in the complicated statements about consciousness, art, and imagination. With these interactions we must be very careful. But there are few major artists whose emotional appeals are so direct and unambiguous, and whose favorites are so obviously meant to awe us with their heroics of deed and perception.

There is abundant mystery in Nabokov's work, but there is no major ambiguity: not about human character, not about good and evil, not about esthetic differences, not about political dynamics. These things are clear and resolved in his work, and the paradoxes with which he is concerned are perhaps epitomized in the terrifying absurdity of having these "riches of consciousness" encased in fragile, mortal bodies. The perceptual consciousness seems so miraculous to Nabokov that he cannot reconcile himself to its being suddenly, banally taken away, and this fact is the grain of sand about which his favorites spin their nacreous fantasies. Van Veen reads his lines well when he proclaims at Aqua's death that "we must always remember that the strength, the dignity, the delight of man is to spite and despise the shadows and stars that hide their secrets from us" (29–30).

Everywhere in Nabokov there is a direct sense of wonder at the perceiving consciousness, and his concerns are with the ecstatic possibilities and hideous limitations of this consciousness. His fictional favorites not only "spite and despise," they contrive subjective solutions to the objective absurdity, alchemize imaginative layers of pearl about that awful grain of brute fact.

Nabokov's poem "The Ballad of Longwood Glen" is an almost perfect paradigm crystallizing the impulses of his fictional favorites: it is, like *Ada,* a version of that happily-ever-after which was promised us somewhere and somehow in an immortal fairytale but which, we come to realize, time and death will deny us. Instead of "where are . . . ?" Nabokov asks "what if . . . ?"

Art Longwood, "a local florist," with his children, wife, father, stepfather, and father-in-law—not a very promising group— arrive at an unnamed glen for a picnic, a blank, bright opening to the conventional American-burgher Sunday with the family. But of course Nabokov must make evident something unendurable in that scene, for his interest is in transcending it:

> Pauline had asthma, Paul used a crutch.
> They were cute little rascals but could not run much.

And so they represent all the failed and miserable facts of this world—the same "reality" that Kinbote must escape.[1] Cautiously, Nabokov sets up his trajectory. Just as he has Ferdinand discard that inkwell before abandoning Nina to time and death in "Spring in Fialta," he gives us a small precursor of the larger action that will follow, and subtly, almost subliminally, alerts our expectations:

> Silent Art, who could stare at a thing all day,
> Watched a bug climb a stalk and fly away.

If one has to be a petit bourgeois in Nabokov's codified cosmos, it is a good thing to be a petit bourgeois florist: flowers and earth, beauty, and silence, growth and symmetry; and this florist has patience and curiosity—certainly positive traits. But the world of vulgar fact makes its demands on Art Longwood, just as it makes them on Vasili in "Cloud, Castle, Lake":

> "I wish," said his mother to crippled Paul,
> "Some man would teach you to pitch that ball."

But there is nothing to be done with this world. Paul is crippled. There is no way to repair the defective and the ugly. Hazel Shade has discovered this, too, and has taken the only solution open to her. Nabokovian favorites don't face up, they face away, to fantasy, escape, suicide. Art dutifully throws the ball up, but it stays in a "passing tree."

> "I never climbed trees in my timid prime,"
> Thought Art; and forthwith started to climb.

He climbs higher; the leaves "said *yes* to the questioning wind," and up in the tree Art thinks "How easy flight," and then flies away.

> None saw the delirious celestial crowds
> Greet the hero from earth in the snow of the clouds.

So much for Art Longwood. He has escaped: "He never came down. He never returned."

But those who do stay down display the hectic animation and heartless vulgarity of those for whom Nabokov has neither pity nor admiration: "Conventioners, fishermen, freckled boys," try to find Art in the tree, "all kinds of humans" mill about, even a lyncher arrives with "a rope and a gun"; the oak is felled and examined—with Artless results.

> They varnished the stump, put up railings and signs.
> Restrooms nestled in roses and vines.
> Mrs. Longwood, retouched, when the children died,
> Became a photographer's dreamy bride.

Mrs. Longwood's indifference to her husband's disappearance and her children's deaths is really no more "irresponsible" than Art's transcendent escape: she is indifferent to fact, which is why she can live with her defective children and survive their death. But we should remember that the value that legitimizes Art Longwood's impulse to escape is distinctly Nabokovian. The annihilating fact, to the scrupulous conscience and sensitive consciousness of a Nabokovian favorite, is much more powerful than any countervailing sense of responsibility and endurance. Nabokov shows no sign of disapproval or even qualification of this impulse to escape; there is no median way in Nabokov's world: "no conscience and hence no consciousness" can survive the ugly facts. Only the lobotomized can endure asthma, crippling, the shanties of Coalmont, the decapitation of Cincinnatus, the destruction of Krug's son, Yasha's suicide, the shooting of Shade, Nina's destruction; only the insensitive can see as "wonderful" romanticism the idea that the history of man is the history of pain, or call attention to a suicided patient's posture as resembling, by Jove, the *fetus-in-utero*. The master impulse for all of

Nabokov's favorites is escape: an escape must be discovered or, if an escape cannot be discovered, it must be invented. Those discoveries and inventions Nabokov has painted for us with the most durable of pigments.

Notes

Page references in brackets or parentheses are to the following editions of Nabokov's fiction: *Bend Sinister*, Time-Life Books, 1964; *Pale Fire*, Putnam's, 1962; *Pnin*, Doubleday, 1957; *The Annotated Lolita*, ed. Alfred Appel, Jr., McGraw-Hill, 1970; *Ada*, McGraw-Hill, 1969. Page numbers for the short stories "Cloud, Castle, Lake" and "Spring in Fialta" refer to the collection *The Portable Nabokov*, edited by Page Stegner, Viking, 1968. "Triangle within Circle" appeared as a short story in *The New Yorker* for March 23, 1963, and can be found on pages 54–62 of *The Gift*. All other quotations are identified by footnote.

Introduction: Nabokov's Constants

1. Vladimir Nabokov, *The Gift* (New York: Putnam's, 1963), p. 39.

2. "Prospero's Progress," *Time*, 69 (May 23, 1969), p. 82.

3. Vladimir Nabokov, *Speak, Memory*, rev. ed. (New York: Pyramid, 1968), p. 219.

4. Vladimir Nabokov, *Bend Sinister* (New York: Time-Life Books, 1964), p. 87.

5. *Ibid.*, p. 209.

6. *Speak, Memory*, p. 14.

7. *Ibid.*, p. 214.

8. *Bend Sinister,* p. xvii.

9. *"Playboy* Interview: Vladimir Nabokov," *Playboy,* 11 (Jan. 1964), 40. Hereafter cited as *Playboy* Interview.

10. L. S. Dembo, ed., *Nabokov: The Man and His Work* (Madison: The University of Wisconsin Press, 1967), p. 22. Hereafter cited as *Dembo.*

11. Vladimir Nabokov, *The Waltz Invention* (New York: Phaedra, 1966), p. 7.

1. The Nabokov Paradigm: *Bend Sinister*

1. *Speak, Memory,* p. 226.

2. *Dembo,* p. 33.

3. *Speak, Memory,* pp. 13–14.

4. *Ibid.,* p. 14.

5. Donald Malcolm, "A Retrospect," *The New Yorker,* 40 (April 25, 1964), 198, 201.

6. *Speak, Memory,* p. 37.

7. Robert M. Adams, "Fiction Chronicle," *Hudson Review,* 15 (*Autumn* 1962), 423.

8. *Speak, Memory,* p. 92.

9. Martin Green, "The Morality of *Lolita,*" *Kenyon Review,* 28 (June 1966), 359, 361.

10. *Playboy* Interview, p. 40.

11. Leo Tolstoy, *What Is Art?,* quoted in Martin Green's "The Morality of *Lolita,*" *Kenyon Review,* 28 (June 1966), 356.

12. Frank Kermode, "Aesthetic Bliss," *Encounter,* 14 (June 1962), 85.

13. L. L. Lee, *"Bend Sinister:* Nabokov's Political Dream," in *Dembo,* p. 100.

14. Vladimir Nabokov, *Nikolai Gogol* (New York: New Directions, 1944), p. 22.

15. *Ibid.,* p. 133.

16. *Ibid.,* p. 150.

17. *Speak, Memory,* p. 92.
18. *Nikolai Gogol,* p. 13.
19. *Ibid.,* p. 149.
20. *Playboy* Interview, p. 40.
21. Vladimir Nabokov, *The Eye* (New York: Phaedra, 1965),
p. ix.
22. *Playboy* Interview, p. 45.
23. *Ibid.,* p. 40.

2. Nabokov's Short Fiction
1. Vladimir Nabokov, *Despair,* rev. ed. (New York: Putnam's,
1966), p. 84.
2. Andrew Field, *Nabokov: His Life in Art* (Boston: Little,
Brown, 1967), p. 197.
3. *Despair,* p. 170.
4. Barbara Heldt Monter, " 'Spring in Fialta': The Choice That
Mimics Chance," in Alfred A. Appel, Jr., and Charles Newman
(eds.), *Nabokov* (New York: Simon and Schuster, 1970), p. 132.
Cited here after as *Appel and Newman.*
5. *The Gift,* pp. 351–352.
6. Julian Moynahan, *"Lolita* and Related Memories," in *Appel
and Newman,* p. 251.
7. Ross Wetzsteon, "Nabokov as Teacher," in *Appel and Newman,* p. 242.
8. *Speak, Memory,* pp. 86–87.
9. *The Gift,* p. 54. The story appears on pp. 54–62. It was published as a short story in *The New Yorker,* March 23, 1963, and
reprinted in *The Portable Nabokov* (New York: Viking, 1971).

3. *Pale Fire*
1. Robert M. Adams, "Fiction Chronicle," *Hudson Review,* 15
(Autumn 1962), 421.

2. John O. Lyons, *"Pale Fire* and the Fine Art of Annotation," in *Dembo,* p. 163–164.

3. Nina Berberova, "The Mechanics of *Pale Fire,"* in *Appel and Newman,* p. 148.

4. *Playboy* Interview, p. 45.

5. *Speak, Memory,* p. 194.

6. Martin Green, "The Morality of *Lolita,"* *Kenyon Review,* 28 (June 1966), p. 352.

7. *Playboy* Interview, p. 44.

8. T. S. Eliot, "Tradition and the Individual Talent," *The Sacred Wood* (London: Methuen, 1920), p. 53.

9. T. S. Eliot, *Collected Poems, 1909–1962* (New York: Harcourt Brace Jovanovich, 1963).

10. Alfred Appel, Jr., "Nabokov: A Portrait," *Atlantic,* 228 (Sept. 1971), 91.

11. *Ibid.,* p. 84.

12. John Crowe Ransom, *Selected Poems* (New York: Knopf, 1963), p. 11.

13. Mary McCarthy, "A Bolt from the Blue," *New Republic,* 146 (June 4, 1962), 26.

14. Herbert Gold, "Reminiscence," in *Appel and Newman,* p. 339.

15. *Speak, Memory,* p. 220.

4. *Pnin*

1. *Dembo,* p. 38.

2. *Playboy* Interview, p. 36.

3. "V.V." also stands for both Van Veen and V. V. Nabokov in *Ada.*

4. Vladimir Nabokov, "Rowe's Symbols," *New York Review of Books* (Oct. 7, 1971), 8.

5. *Lolita*

1. Martin Green, "The Morality of *Lolita*," *Kenyon Review*, 28 (June 1966), 365.

2. *Ibid.*, p. 357.

3. Van Veen tells his Ada that they feel exhilarated as their affair progresses at Ardis Hall because their nerves are alive with danger and their successful mastering of it: they are "two spies in an alien country." Antiterra, however, is neither alien nor dangerous enough to give this much force, as we shall see.

4. Martin Green, *Re-Appraisals: Some Commonsense Readings in American Literature* (New York: Norton, 1965), p. 215.

5. Nabokov's poem "The Ballad of Longwood Glen," discussed in the Epilogue, is another example of the triumph of indifference.

6. That "mirror" in *Pale Fire* might be the *trompe l'oeil* construct described by Kinbote in Onhava Palace: in depicting a "Count Kernal," the court painter Eystein emblemized the good soldier's name by depicting the man with "a plate with the beautifully executed, twin-lobed, brainlike, halved kernel of a walnut" on it, and a real bronze drawer insert on the side. The revolutionaries who have interned Kinbote in searching for the crown jewels open the real drawer and it contains "nothing, however, except the broken bits of a nutshell" (130). Perhaps this image, more than any other, represents the novel's complex interchange of the "real" and the "artificial." Alfred Appel, Jr., finds the image of the small convex mirror suggestive, too, but chooses to apply it as a metaphor to different aspects of *Lolita*. See *The Annotated Lolita* (McGraw-Hill, 1970), p. 359.

7. Humbert and Lolita later attend a performance of a play called *The Lady Who Loved Lightning* co-authored by Quilty and a "Vivian Darkbloom." This obvious authorial anagram is perhaps Nabokov's signal to us of the importance of *The Enchanted Hunters:* Quilty is gifted enough to work with the local Daedalus.

8. Included in *The Portable Nabokov*, edited by Page Stegner (New York: Viking, 1971), pp. 199–212.

9. *Ibid.*, pp. 172–178.
10. *Dembo*, p. 28.

6. *Ada*

1. Vladimir Nabokov, "Letters," *New York Review of Books,* 13 (July 10, 1969), 36.

2. Onegin's duel with Lenski forms the most exciting passage in *Eugene Onegin;* in his Commentary, Nabokov points out that Pushkin had "been out" at least three times before his fatal meeting with d'Anthes. Two of these were military men. Evidently the excitement intrigued Nabokov so much he had to try one of his own, at least in fiction.

3. Alfred Appel, Jr., *"Ada* Described," in *Appel and Newman,* p. 181.

4. Robert Alter, "Nabokov's Ardor," *Commentary,* 48 (Aug. 1969), 49.

5. *Speak, Memory,* p. 139.

6. Nabokov acknowledges his changes in this manner: "Two chess games with identical opening and identical end moves might ramify in an infinite number of variations on *one* board and in *two* brains [that is, Antiterra and Terra], at any middle stage of the irrevocably converging development" (19). But the alterations made on Antiterra aren't arbitrary: they conform to Nabokov's predilections.

7. In his short story "Time and Ebb," an old scientist soliloquizes on the strange quiddity of the twentieth century. In keeping with Nabokov's sense of the imminence of an enormous revelation or horrifying discovery, the speaker mentions the "staggering discoveries" of the 1970's—evidently so staggering that all flying devices have been outlawed, just as electricity and flying carpets have been outlawed on Antiterra. He also tells us that creatures of the twentieth century "played with electricity without having the slightest notion of what it really was—and no wonder the chance revelation

of its true nature came as a most hideous surprise (I was a man at the time and can well remember old Professor Andrews sobbing his heart out on the campus in the midst of a dumbfounded crowd)." Discovery and shock are forms of energy Nabokov always keeps close at hand in his work, whether they involve Krug's fictitiousness, Kinbote's madness, or Quilty's identity. They are the means by which Nabokov attempts to recreate that "stab of wonder" which we experience at finding brilliant mimicry in nature, the master mimic.

8. *The Gift,* p. 212.

9. There are about twenty references to Cindrella in *Ada,* most of them connected with the maid Blanche at Ardis Hall. (In *Bend Sinister,* this micro-motif appears only about a half-dozen times.) We not only have Blanche dressed in a "miniver" coat—*menu* plus *vair* in Old French meant "small fur," which we specialists remember from *Pnin* as being the real material of Cinderella's slipper—but we even find Blanche being delivered back to Ardis Hall in a "pumpkin-hued police van" long after midnight. In almost every respect, *Ada* is Nabokov's boldest reincarnation and recapitulation of his life-long predilections, discoveries, and insights. For example, we hear several times, apropos of nothing in particular, that Tolstoy, not Joyce, was the progenitor of the interior monologue. This statement and others like it give the novel its textbook air.

7. Epilogue: "The Ballad of Longwood Glen"

1. Mrs. Richard Schiller and her partially deaf husband are accompanied by a crippled (one-armed) friend in Coalmont. Humbert, his mind on a great deal else, does have time to comment on the man's prideful puncture which he suffers opening a beer can: "It was then noticed that one of the few thumbs remaining to Bill was bleeding (not such a wonder worker after all)," and Humbert wonders if Lolita's beauty does not "excite the cripple." Dick must be shouted to, and misinterprets one shout to inform Humbert that

Bill lost his arm in Italy. Humbert has a vision: "Lovely mauve almond trees in bloom. A blown-off surrealistic arm hanging up there in pointillistic mauve." If one remembers that the Coalmont scene is Nabokov's sole presentation of lower-middle-class American life, the heavy emphasis on defectiveness is unavoidably suggestive of Nabokov's despair with the nonpossibilities of this life. It is all so hopeless that Humbert's offer to Lo to "live happily ever after" with him is, I think, only rhetorical: Nabokov could never let them come back together, for she is too much at home with cripples and Coalmont, and both she and Humbert are assumed into an artificial death that is no less a fairytale than a happily-ever-after would be.

Bibliography

Adams, Robert M. "Fiction Chronicle." *Hudson Review,* 15 (Autumn 1962), 420–430.

Amis, Kingsley, "She was a Child and I was a Child." *Spectator* (Nov. 6, 1959), pp. 633–636.

Appel, Alfred, Jr., ed. *The Annotated Lolita.* New York: McGraw-Hill, 1970.

———. "Nabokov: A Portrait." *Atlantic,* 228 (Sept. 1971), 77–79, 83–85, 88, 91–92.

———, and Charles Newman, eds. *Nabokov.* Evanston: Northwestern University Press, 1970; rpt. New York: Simon and Schuster, 1970.

Chester, Alfred. "Nabokov's Anti-Novel." *Commentary,* 34 (Nov. 1962), 449–451.

Dembo, L. S., ed. *Nabokov: The Man and His Work.* Madison: University of Wisconsin, 1967.

Dupee, F. W. "The Coming of Nabokov." *The King of the Cats and Other Remarks on Writers and Writing.* New York: Farrar, Straus and Giroux (1965), pp. 117–141.

Duval-Smith, Peter. "Vladimir Nabokov on His Life and Work." *The Listener,* 68 (Nov. 22, 1962), pp. 856–858.

Eliot, T. S. *Collected Poems, 1909–1962.* New York: Harcourt Brace Jovanovich; and London: Faber and Faber, 1963.

———. *The Sacred Wood.* London: Methuen, 1920.

Fiedler, Leslie A. *Love and Death in the American Novel.* Rev. ed. New York: Dell (1966), pp. 334–335, 419.

Field, Andrew. "The Defenseless Luzhin." *On Contemporary Literature.* Edited by Richard Kostelanetz. New York: Avon (1964), pp. 473–476.

———. *Nabokov: His Life in Art.* Boston: Little, Brown, 1967.

Green, Martin. "American Rococo: Salinger and Nabokov." *Re-Appraisals: Some Commonsense Readings in American Literature.* New York: Norton (1965), pp. 211–229.

———. "The Morality of *Lolita.*" *Kenyon Review,* 28 (June 1966), 352–377.

Hodgart, Matthew. "Happy Families." *New York Review of Books,* May 22, 1969, p. 3.

Hollander, John. "The Perilous Magic of Nymphets." *Partisan Review,* 23 (Fall, 1956), 557–560. Rpt. in Richard Kostelanetz, *On Contemporary Literature.* New York: Avon (1964), pp. 477–480.

Karlinsky, Simon. "Nabokov's Russian Games." *New York Times Book Review,* April 18, 1971, p. 3.

Kermode, Frank. "Aesthetic Bliss." *Encounter,* 14 (June 1960), 81–86.

———. "Zemblances." *New Statesman,* 64 (Nov. 9, 1962), 671–672.

McCarthy, Mary. "A Bolt From the Blue." *New Republic,* 146 (June 4, 1962), 21–27.

MacDonald, Dwight. "Virtuosity Rewarded or Dr. Kinbote's Revenge." *Partisan Review,* 29 (Summer 1962), 437–442.

Malcolm, Donald. "A Retrospect." *The New Yorker,* 40 (April 25, 1964), 198, 201, 202–205.

Maloff, Saul. "The World of Rococo." *Nation,* 194 (June 16, 1962), 541–542.

Moynahan, Julian. "Speaking of Books: Vladimir Nabokov." *New York Times Book Review,* April 3, 1966, pp. 2, 14.

Nabokov, Vladimir. *Ada or Ardor: A Family Chronicle.* New York: McGraw-Hill, 1969.

——. *Bend Sinister*. New York: Holt, 1947; rpt. with author's introduction, New York: Time Reading Program, 1964.

——. *The Defense*. New York: Putnam's, 1964.

——. *Despair*. Rev. ed. New York: Putnam's, 1966.

——. *The Eye*. New York: Phaedra, 1965.

——. *The Gift*. New York: Putnam's, 1963.

——. *Invitation to a Beheading*. New York: Putnam's, 1959; rpt. New York: Crest, 1960.

——. *Lolita*. New York: McGraw-Hill, 1970.

——. *Nabokov's Dozen: A Collection of Thirteen Stories*. New York: Doubleday, 1958.

——. *Nabokov's Quartet*. New York: Phaedra, 1966.

——. *Nikolai Gogol*. Rev. ed. 1961. New York: New Directions, 1944.

——. *Pale Fire*. New York: Putnam's, 1962.

——. *Pnin*. New York: Doubleday, 1957.

——. *Poems and Problems*. New York: McGraw-Hill, 1970.

——. *Speak, Memory: A Memoir Revisited*. Rev. ed. New York: Pyramid, 1968.

——. *The Waltz Invention: A Play in Three Acts*. New York: Phaedra, 1966.

Nemerov, Howard. "The Morality of Art" and "The Ills from Missing Dates," *Poetry and Fiction: Essays*. New Brunswick, N.J.: Rutgers (1963), pp. 260–269.

"*Playboy* Interview: Vladimir Nabokov." *Playboy*, 11 (Jan. 1964), pp. 35–41, 44–45.

"Pnin & Pen." *Time*, 69 (March 18, 1957), 108, 110.

"Prospero's Progress." *Time*, 76 (May 23, 1969).

Pryce-Jones, Alan. "The Fabulist's Worlds: Vladimir Nabokov." *The Creative Present—Notes on Contemporary American Fiction*. Edited by Nona Balakian and Charles Simmons. Garden City: Doubleday (1963), pp. 65–78.

Ransom, John Crowe. *Selected Poems*. New York: Knopf, 1963.

Stegner, Page. *Escape into Aesthetics: The Art of Vladimir Nabokov.* New York: Dial, 1966.

——, ed. *The Portable Nabokov.* New York: Viking, 1971.

Trilling, Lionel. "The Last Lover—Vladimir Nabokov's 'Lolita,' " *Griffin,* 7 (Aug. 1958), 4–21. Rpt. in *Encounter,* 11 (Oct. 1958), 9–19.

Updike, John. "Nabokov's Look Back: A National Loss." *Life,* 62 (Jan. 13, 1967), 11, 15.

Index

DATE DUE

DEMCO 38-297